SOUTHERN HOMES AND PLAN BOOKS

Southern Homes & Plan Books

THE ARCHITECTURAL LEGACY OF LEILA ROSS WILBURN

Sarah J. Boykin and Susan M. Hunter

The University of Georgia Press   *Athens*

A Wormsloe
FOUNDATION
PUBLICATION

© 2018 by the University of Georgia Press
Athens, Georgia 30602
www.ugapress.org
All rights reserved
Designed by Erin Kirk New
Set in Adobe Garamond Pro
Printed and bound by Four Colour Print Group

The paper in this book meets the guidelines for permanence and
durability of the Committee on Production Guidelines for
Book Longevity of the Council on Library Resources.

Most University of Georgia Press titles are available from
popular e-book vendors.

Printed in China
22 21 20 19 18 C 5 4 3 2 1

Library of Congress Cataloging-in-Publication Data

Names: Boykin, Sarah J., author. | Hunter, Susan M., 1936– author.
Title: Southern homes and plan books : the architectural legacy of
    Leila Ross Wilburn / Sarah J. Boykin and Susan M. Hunter.
Description: Athens : The University of Georgia Press, 2018. | Includes
    bibliographical references and index.
Identifiers: LCCN 2018008660 | ISBN 9780820351810 (hardback : alk. paper)
Subjects: LCSH: Wilburn, Leila Ross, 1885–1967—Criticism and
    interpretation. | Architecture, Domestic—Southern States—Designs
    and plans. | Pattern books—Southern States.
Classification: LCC NA737.W5237 B69 2018 | DDC 720.92—dc23
LC record available at https://lccn.loc.gov/2018008660

Frontispiece: House designed by Leila Ross Wilburn and built in the
McDonough–Adams–King's Highway (MAK) Historic District from
plan design no. 655, which was published in *Southern Homes and
Bungalows* (1914).

CONTENTS

LIST OF PLAN BOOKS AND PUBLICATIONS

This list of Leila Ross Wilburn's known plan book publications includes nine plan books and five smaller offprints. Each of the nine plan books was sold as a catalogue containing fifty to one hundred mail-order house plans that could be purchased and ordered from Wilburn. The smaller offprints had fewer designs and were promotional publications, often printed for builders to offer as select house designs for their clients.

Plan Books

1. *Southern Homes and Bungalows.* 82 designs. 1914. 75 cents. This is the only plan book that had a publication date.
2. *Brick and Colonial Homes.* 86 designs. 1921. The date of publication was included in an article in the *Atlanta Constitution*, October 30, 1921. It sold for $2.00.
3. *Ideal Homes of Today.* 100 designs. Circa 1925. $2.00.
4. *Homes in Good Taste.* 53 designs. Circa 1927.
5. *New Homes of Quality.* 62 designs. Circa 1930.
6. *Small Low-Cost Homes for the South.* 62 designs. Circa 1935.
7. *Sixty Good New Homes.* 60 designs. Circa 1938.
8. *Ranch and Colonial Homes.* 63 designs. Circa 1950. $1.00.
9. *Bran-New Homes.* 64 designs. 1960. $1.00.

Booklets and Offprints

"Homes of Individuality." Advertised in the *Atlanta Constitution*, April 1915.

"Up-to-date Homes." 24 designs. Published between 1914 and 1921.

"Successful Homes." 17 designs in free folder. Published between 1914 and 1921.

"One-Story Houses: Selected from My Plan Books *Ideal Homes of Today* and *Brick and Colonial Homes.*" 14 designs. Published circa 1926. This offprint was an advertising booklet that was produced for builders (in quantities of 100) to provide to their customers for selecting a suitable house design.

"New Plans for Home Builders." 18 designs. Published circa 1928.

Leila Ross Wilburn could choose from many models as she prepared her first catalogue to sell house plans, the 1914 *Southern Homes and Bungalows*. Popular magazines of the period carried advertisements for such catalogues in every issue, and magazines of the carpentry and building trades did the same. In addition, retail lumber yards and builders provided catalogues of designs for their customers. Wilburn's emulation of the catalogues of her time is evident in all of her plan books, as well as in the independent choices that she made in specific aspects of their format and in her designs.

The practice of publishing catalogues to sell house designs was not new when Wilburn produced *Southern Homes and Bungalows*, but the number of such catalogues was increasing, and the audience for them was expanding. Architects had published books of their designs for centuries in order to build their reputations and attract clients, but until the nineteenth century such books were directed to the wealthy. When designers began to publish the more modest books of smaller house designs that are now referred to as pattern books, they found a receptive audience in the growing middle class. A. J. Downing, following British examples, authored the earliest successful American pattern books, beginning with *Cottage Residences* in 1842. Pattern books typically devoted one or two pages to each house design, providing an exterior view, floor plans, and descriptive text. Their stated purpose was usually similar to Downing's "hearty desire to contribute something to the improvement of the domestic architecture and the rural taste of our country."[1] Pattern books were not intended to sell plans, but readers wrote

and asked for plans anyway, and it was a natural step for architects to start publishing books for the specific purpose of selling plans.

In 1856 the architectural firm of Cleaveland and Backus included an offer to sell plans in their book *Village and Farm Cottages*, becoming one of the earliest firms to offer mail-order plans. However, brothers George and Charles Palliser were the first in America to find widespread and continuing success from the practice with their catalogues of the 1870s through the 1890s. The success of the Pallisers enticed many competitors to follow them into the field, and the flood of new publications found a ready market. An increased demand for housing certainly contributed to their influence, but the development and building patterns of the time were also key factors. Unlike the developers of today, most developers of neighborhoods intended for single family homes in the late nineteenth and early twentieth centuries were in the business of selling lots, not houses. This meant that aspiring homeowners had a much greater choice in their house designs. Developers surveyed land, laid out streets, and then sold the lots to individuals. Some of those buyers made their purchases for investment, intending to sell later at a profit, and others built one or more houses for speculative sale. However, most of the people buying lots hired builders to construct houses for them according to designs of their choice. They could use a custom house design by a builder or architect, or they could choose a design from a wide range of printed sources—magazine articles, advice books, mail-order catalogues, or lumberyard catalogues.

Mail-order catalogues of house plans resembled the pattern books from which they developed in general but differed in several specific ways. Like pattern books, they provided a perspective view, floor plan, and description for each house design, but the catalogues used less space for each design. Catalogues usually allowed only one page per design and often squeezed two or more on a page, whereas pattern books more often provided two pages for each design and its description. In addition, house plan catalogues over time assumed the format and graphics of general mail-order catalogues. They were produced in all shapes and sizes, with colorful, eye-catching graphics on the covers. The covers themselves were often paper, rather than the hard covers of pattern books. Paper covers and cheaper paper enabled larger print runs and more affordable prices, which meant that the publications could reach more potential customers.

The traditional East Coast publishing centers had no monopoly on catalogues of house plans. Although several early ones were produced in New York City, other prominent examples came from the Midwest and the South. David S. Hopkins published at least eight editions of *Houses and Cottages* in Grand Rapids, Michigan, in the 1880s and 1890s, while Herbert C. Chivers began publishing larger and larger editions of his *Artistic Homes* in St. Louis. (His 1910 edition included 1,500 designs on 1,000 pages!) George F. Barber, based in Knoxville, Tennessee, became one of the most successful mail-order architects of the 1890s and early 1900s.

When the American bungalow became the rage in the first decade of the 1900s, catalogues of bungalow plans, known by the alliterative term "bungalow books," poured out of Los Angeles, where this house type first enjoyed popularity. E. W. Stillwell, Henry L. Wilson, and the imaginatively named firms Ye Planry and Bungalowcraft were among the most successful Los Angeles publishers of bungalow books. Bungalows represented the fresh, informal, healthful approach to living typical of their California birthplace, but designers in other states did not hesitate to jump into the market. Fred T. Hodgson's *Practical Bungalows and Cottages*

(1906) and *Radford's Artistic Bungalows* (1908) were both published in Chicago, and Jud Yoho produced bungalow books in Seattle.

Most publishers of catalogues of house plans still referred to these publications as books, even when they looked like mail-order catalogues. Keith Publishing Company of Minneapolis, Minnesota, advertised its "latest books of plans" in 1901; J. H. Daverman & Son of Grand Rapids, Michigan, promoted their "Book of Plans" in 1907; and E. W. Stillwell of Los Angeles described his *West Coast Bungalows* as an "entirely new book of pictures and plans" in a 1911 advertisement, yet each of these publications had the paper covers and general appearance of a mail-order catalogue.[2] Wilburn followed these precedents when she advertised her first publication in 1914 as a "book of plans." But by 1915 she started using the more concise term "plan book" in later advertisements for the same publication.[3]

The term "plan book" appears to have come into general use in the building trades and retail lumber yards that served them. Early published examples of the term include Burd Miller's *Home Builders Plan Book* (1905), published in Omaha, Nebraska, by Home Builders, Inc., and *Lumberman's House Plan Book* (1907), published in Chicago by Radford Architectural Co. Advertisements using the term appeared in the magazines of the building trade at around the same time. The use of the word "plan" rather than "design" reflects the practical approach of professional builders, who needed detailed plans, including floor plans, elevations, and specifications, to construct a house, rather than pretty designs or perspective views. The term "plan book" also helped to distinguish catalogues that sold plans from ready-cut house catalogues that sold all the building materials for a house in pre-cut form ready for assembly. The Aladdin Company (Bay City, Michigan) published its first ready-cut catalogue in 1906, and Sears Roebuck and Co. (Chicago) published their first in 1908.

Owners and managers of retail lumber yards felt threatened by ready-cut house catalogues, and they began using plan books to encourage customers to buy materials locally from their enterprises rather than from ready-cut companies. Their trade publications featured articles about the mail-order threat with titles such as "Fighting Ready-Cut Houses" and recommendations for displays of plan books in retail lumber yards. The lumber company William Cameron & Co. contracted with Ye Planry in 1915 to supply thirty-five of the company's lumber yards in the Southwest with plan books. Dallas entrepreneur R. W. Williamson sold a series of plan books to retail lumber yards in Texas, Oklahoma, Arkansas, Louisiana, Missouri, and Illinois.[4] Trade associations also joined the plan book chorus. The Southern Pine Association, headquartered in New Orleans, commissioned and published plan books for distribution to lumber yards, including *Modern Homes* (1921) and *Southern Pine Homes* (1924).

Wilburn may have picked up her use of the term "plan book" from examples advertised in magazines or displayed in lumber yards, but the physical appearance and arrangement of her books show her awareness of a full range of house design catalogues. In her first book, *Southern Homes and Bungalows* (1914), she opted for a vertical format (11 inches by 8.5 inches) that was used in such varied catalogues as *Radford's Artistic Homes* (1908), Henry L. Wilson's *Bungalow Book* (1910), and Gustav Stickley's *More Craftsman Homes* (1912), rather than the smaller, horizontal format used in *Ye Planry Bungalows* (1911), *"The Draughtsman" Bungalows* (1913), and the Sears Roebuck ready-cut house catalogues of this period. Wilburn did not switch to a horizontal format until the 1930s.

Every publisher of a house plan catalogue had to address the thorny issue of whether to include estimated construction costs with their designs. Many included the costs, for consumers appreciated knowing how much a design would cost them to build. Contractors and builders, however, disapproved of the practice. Costs of materials and labor varied around the country and often increased during the months, or years, between a catalogue's publication and the time the consumer might decide on a plan. Builders did not like being blamed when they could not match prices quoted in catalogues.[5] Wilburn sided with the builders in this

matter. In her first catalogue Wilburn did not include construction costs, but she offered to supply them upon request. In her 1921 catalogue, she declined to do even that. Instead, she instructed her readers that "the cost question for years will be more or less problematical. . . . Select the plan you desire to build . . . and have your contractor give you a bid for the completed job."[6]

Wilburn showed similar independence when she used only photographic halftone illustrations of the houses in her 1914 plan book. Most catalogues used a combination of photographs and perspective drawings. By using perspective drawings, the publishers of these catalogues were able to include designs that might not have been built yet. Wilburn began including perspective drawings along with photographs in her 1921 plan book.

Wilburn also differed from other plan book architects through the simple fact of her gender. Very few women practiced architecture in the early twentieth century, and even fewer published books of house designs. Emily Elizabeth Holman of Philadelphia was the major exception before Wilburn. Holman published at least six catalogues between 1900 and 1910, but she effectively disguised her gender by giving only her first initials in her publications. Wilburn, in contrast, used her gender as a selling point for her plans and used her full name. As she wrote in *Brick and Colonial Homes* in 1921, "I feel that, being a woman, I know just the little things that should go in a house to make living in it a pleasure to the entire family."[7]

As with the format and presentation of her plan books, Wilburn's house designs display her awareness and use of national design trends as well as adjustments to floor plans and interior spaces to create residences appropriate for the American South. Although the illustrations of bungalows and two-story houses that she designed do not appear significantly different from those in other plan books of the period, they demonstrate her ability to develop a market by promoting her work as a southern designer. The following chapters address her designs in detail as well as her desire, as stated in her first book, to design homes "suitable for climatic conditions of the Southeast."[8] Although Wilburn's sleeping porches appear to be one of those southern adaptations, sleeping porches actually emerged nationally as a preventive measure against tuberculosis in the early twentieth century. They first gained prominence in America in the late nineteenth century as part of the treatment for tuberculosis, but soon doctors were recommending fresh-air sleeping as a preventive measure as well as treatment for tuberculosis. By 1908 the popular press acknowledged the increasing prevalence of outdoor sleeping for health and promoted the practice through articles in such periodicals as *Country Life in America* and *House Beautiful*, as well as in general health manuals.[9]

In the early 1920s a sleeping porch was accepted as an important component of any proper middle-class home, whether it be in Georgia or Minnesota. The title character in Sinclair Lewis's novel *Babbitt*, published in 1922, was as proud of the sleeping porch in his up-to-date home as of his ability to sleep on it on all but the coldest of nights.[10] However, house catalogues of the time provide some evidence that sleeping porches may have been more prevalent in the warmer parts of the country than in the North, in spite of the pronouncements and recommendations found in the media. Wilburn's plan books contribute to that evidence. The 1918 Sears Roebuck catalogue, published in Chicago, included sleeping porches in 12 percent of its house designs, and the 1925 *Beautiful Homes* published by Keith Corporation in Minneapolis included them in 23 percent. In contrast, 40 percent of the designs in the Southern Pine Association's 1921 catalogue included sleeping porches, and 60 percent of the designs in Wilburn's 1921 catalogue *Brick and Colonial Homes* did so.

The 1930s presented serious challenges to architects, builders, and publishers of plan books, including Wilburn. The Great Depression shattered the housing construction industry until the later years of the decade, when Federal Housing Administration programs helped support a partial recovery. War-related shortages of building materials and labor created more difficulties in the 1940s. When house construction began to rebound in the late 1940s, large-scale developer-builders, including William Levitt, transformed building patterns. They offered their customers only a limited selection of stock plans for houses in their developments. Many publishers of plan books gave up during those years, but Wilburn published three plan books in the 1930s, one around 1950, and a final one around 1960. With these publications, she proved her amazing persistence, as well as her ability to adapt to changing design trends and market forces.

Surprisingly little is known about the individuals responsible for thousands of house designs published in catalogues and plan books during the first three decades of the twentieth century, with the notable exception of Gustav Stickley, the designer who published the magazine *The Craftsman* (1901–1916) and the books *Craftsman Homes* (1909) and *More Craftsman Homes* (1912). Even with the well-known and documented Sears Roebuck & Co. house catalogues, information about the people actually responsible for the designs remains minimal. The work of Boykin and Hunter helps to fill the gap by providing an unusually detailed study of the career of a significant plan book architect. For most of the plan book architects of the period, we have almost no published evidence of their work or of their lives beyond the designs in their books. In addition, examples of uncredited "borrowed" designs appear with some frequency among the catalogues and magazines, leaving the identities of the original designers even more uncertain. It is to be hoped that more researchers will follow the example of Boykin and Hunter to search for records and documentation of other plan book architects and to produce similar studies. The combined results would enable a deeper understanding of the design world responsible for the historic neighborhoods of the era that we treasure today.

Leila Ross Wilburn's plan books enabled her to survive and prosper as an architect over a span of more than fifty years. Those same plan books now enable the study and appreciation of her long and fruitful career, as shown on the following pages of this book.

ACKNOWLEDGMENTS

In researching Wilburn's architectural designs, documenting her plan book houses, and writing her story, we were inspired by Wilburn, most of all. As an architect, Leila Ross Wilburn celebrated the everyday and the practical, insisting on beauty and craftsmanship, utility and affordability, efficiency and comfort. In designing a number of notable Atlanta apartment buildings and supplying homeowners and builders throughout the Southeast with mail-order plan designs, Wilburn created a rich architectural legacy that includes the hundreds of homes built from her nine plan books.

As the first book-length publication on Leila Ross Wilburn, *Southern Homes and Plan Books: The Architectural Legacy of Leila Ross Wilburn* represents many years of research, discoveries, and findings that have increased our knowledge and understanding of her work, her life, and her legacy, particularly her plan book houses in the Atlanta area. Although we claim this book as our own with all of its limitations and imperfections, we are profoundly grateful for the support from individuals far and near, whose expertise, knowledge, generosity, and kindness have contributed in immeasurable ways. The list is long and continues to grow. We thank them all:

Historians, scholars, authors, and archivists, whose work has informed and enriched our own, especially: Catherine W. Bishir, Clifford Edward Clark Jr., Richard Cloues, Doris Cole, Robert M. Craig, Margaret Culbertson, the late Franklin M. Garrett, Alan Gowans, Dolores Hayden, Jan Jennings, Miriam Mathura, Virginia Savage McAlester, David Ramsey, Daniel D. Reiff, Kenneth Thomas, and Gwendolyn Wright.

Homeowners and residents of Wilburn-designed homes, with appreciation and gratitude for all who have shared stories, offered insights, and welcomed us into their homes, especially: Marianne and John Busby, Yovy Gonzalez and Mike Dorsey, Doc and Marci Nunnery, Scott Simpson and Eric Vaughn, Leisa and Lyman Wray.

Libraries, archives, preservation centers, and their staff: the Kenan Research Center at the Atlanta History Center, especially Helen Matthews and Jena Jones; the Atlanta Urban Design Commission; the McCain Library Special Collections & Archives at Agnes Scott College, especially Marianne Bradley; the Georgia State Historic Preservation Center; the Atlanta-Fulton Public Library; the DeKalb History Center; the Georgia Institute of Technology Library; the Historic Preservation Division of Georgia Department of Natural Resources, especially Christy Atkins; the Hargrett Rare Book and Manuscript Library at the University of Georgia; and the Woodruff Library at Emory University.

Research assistant Catalina Oliver, whose many contributions as a summer intern in 2014 are much appreciated.

Leila Ross Wilburn's relatives, for their many contributions and remembrances about their Aunt Lee and the Wilburn family, especially: Wilburn's niece, the late Elizabeth (Lib) Frierson Kennedy, who provided stories as well as photographs that expanded our understanding of Wilburn's life and work; Wilburn's niece, Catherine Wilburn Carter; great-niece Jean Kennedy Dantzler; nephew Joseph Wilburn III; great-nephew Joseph Wilburn IV; and her sister, the late Llewellyn Wilburn, for her gift of the Leila Ross Wilburn Collection, given to Susan M. Hunter to donate to the Atlanta History Center in the 1970s, and whose 1978 family history provided invaluable information about the family.

Sarah Boykin thanks her family, friends, and colleagues, for good times, wise counsel, and steadfast support along the way, especially: Lynn and John Adams, Anne S. Boykin and the late Rev. Elmer M. Boykin, Anne Boykin-Smith and Struan R. Smith, Lyn and James Bradford, Linda Collins, Carol Elliott, Anne and Clay Preston, Mary Rosenbaum, Lillian Smith, Sarah Smith, Tyler Smith, Lee Stapleton, Leonard Thibadeau, Merissa Tobler and Jim Peterman, and Margaret Winters.

Sarah also thanks organizers and participants of the following conferences, for the opportunities to deliver presentations on Leila Ross Wilburn's architectural legacy and for their interests in her work: "Reclaiming Women's History through Historic Preservation," at Bryn Mawr College in 1994; "Telling Her Story, Expanding the Past of Georgia's Women through Historic Places," at Agnes Scott College in 1996; "The Vernacular Architecture Forum (VAF) Annual Meeting," in Washington, D.C., in 2011; and "The Southeast Society of Architectural Historians (SESAH) Annual Meeting," in Charleston, S.C., in 2011.

Susan Hunter would like to thank her friends, colleagues, and family for their unfailing support over many decades: Renee Brown-Bryant, Erika Danylchek, Marianne DeHaan, Julia Emmons, Katherine Farnham, Diann Kayah, Mary Caroline Lindsay, Pam Porter, Pat Shropshire, Jean Stroman, Judy Tabb; her children Daryl O'Hare, Howard Smith, Steve Smith, and their wonderful spouses; and her grandchildren Aidan O'Hare, Kira O'Hare, Ansley Smith, Carson Smith, Davis Smith, and Isabelle Smith.

Leila Ross Wilburn *Professional Beginnings and Family Life*

Leila Ross Wilburn was born in Macon, Georgia, in 1885, and she opened her own architectural office in Atlanta in 1908, at the age of twenty-three. Throughout her career, which lasted more than five decades, she addressed the need for smaller, more economical homes for the middle class by supplying builders and developers with house designs and by publishing many of her designs in plan books. Wilburn's nine plan books—beginning with the 1914 publication *Southern Homes and Bungalows*—offered mail-order house plans from which prospective homeowners and builders could select and purchase drawings and specifications for construction. Each plan book contained designs that were ready to be built from drawings and specifications that were a fraction of the cost of custom designs. Wilburn's prolific career as a plan book architect included the publication of nine large plan books from which mail-order house plans were purchased to build southern homes throughout the Southeast. Throughout her career she also took on some custom commissions and non-residential work.

The oldest child of Joseph Gustavus Wilburn (b. 1851) and Leila Ada Ross Wilburn (b. 1855), Leila Ross Wilburn was born on November 18, 1885. She was raised in Macon, Georgia, the hometown of her parents, with her three younger siblings, Alice (b. 1888), Joseph (b. 1890), and Walter Ross (b. 1894), until the mid-1890s. At that time, the Wilburn family moved to Atlanta, where Wilburn's sister, Llewellyn, was born in 1898.

Wilburn's parents had grown up in large southern families and married in Macon in 1880. Her mother's family, the Rosses, had settled in Macon after moving from North Carolina in the early 1800s. Her mother, Leila Ada Ross, the youngest of eight children, received her college degree from Wesleyan Female College, a private women's college in Macon, in 1871, and she later studied art in Philadelphia.[1] She is remembered as a talented artist whose beautiful paintings are family treasures. Leila Ross Wilburn's father, Joseph,

FIGURE INT.1.
This photograph of Leila Ross Wilburn as a young woman is one of the few surviving photographs from Wilburn's early years.

FIGURE INT.2. Main Hall, Agnes Scott College, 2014.

FIGURE INT.3. Advertisement for B. R. Padgett & Sons printed in the 1908 *Atlanta City Directory*.

the oldest of six children, attended Mercer University in Macon and was a bookkeeper by profession.[2]

Wilburn attended Agnes Scott Institute, now Agnes Scott College, a private school for women in Decatur, Georgia, from 1902 to 1904. Her coursework included math, history, drawing, and rhetoric, subjects that would have provided knowledge and skills applicable in the practice of architecture. Both Leila Ada Ross and Joseph Wilburn valued education for their children, and in 1904 they moved from Atlanta to Decatur, near to Agnes Scott, where all three of the daughters would receive high-quality educations, as their mother had at Wesleyan Female College.[3] According to a family member, Wilburn's father also had paid for her to take private architectural drafting lessons as a young woman, after he recognized her abilities and interests in developing accurate, precise drawings.

With her Agnes Scott education and her training in drafting and producing architectural drawings to scale, in 1906 Wilburn obtained a job as a draftsperson at B. R. Padgett & Sons, an established architectural and construction firm in Atlanta.[4] At B. R. Padgett & Sons, she likely received additional training and experience in architectural drafting, design and construction.[5] In 1908, she left the firm to open her own architectural office in the Peters Building in downtown Atlanta.[6] This building housed architects, contractors, developers, real estate companies, lawyers, manufacturing representatives (lumber, brick, coal, soda founts, dry goods), and others in the building trades, along with the offices of Edward C. Peters, the building's owner and developer. Wilburn's address gave her immediate access to partners and colleagues, an advantage that would have been extremely beneficial as she built her own practice.

In Wilburn's first years of architectural practice, she had a number of notable commissions for non-residential as well as residential projects.[7] At the same time, Wilburn began providing residential house plans to builders and developers, who were constructing homes in the Atlanta area.

Although Wilburn maintained an office in the Peters Building in downtown Atlanta for her entire career, her home was in Decatur, a historic community six miles east of Atlanta, which had been established in 1823 as a county seat for the newly created DeKalb County.[8] From early in Wilburn's career, her hometown of Decatur claimed her as their own "well-known Decatur architect."[9] In the early twentieth century, Decatur had large parcels of undeveloped land, newly developed subdivisions, a vibrant commercial district, and good public transportation lines, including the Georgia Railroad, which provided a direct and easy commute to downtown Atlanta, then a railroad and commercial center about to enter a period of remarkable growth. However, according to historian Franklin Garrett, before 1908 "Decatur was a rather sleepy small town of 2000 inhabitants" with few of the city services, such as paved roads, water, and sewerage, found in larger urban centers.[10] In 1911, the Decatur Board of Trade was established by private citizens to advocate for public improvements, and the organization's work contributed to a population increase to more than twenty thousand by 1927.[11]

Soon after Wilburn began her own practice, Decatur developers J. W. Mayson and P. L. Weekes purchased property south of College Avenue, on South McDonough Street, Adams Street, and King's Highway down to Oakview Road, with the intention of making this area one of the most desirable subdivisions of new houses in the area. They purchased the land

FIGURE INT.4. The Peters Building, 1947.

in parcels fronting these streets, as well as fronting College Avenue. Most of it was undeveloped, except for the campus of Agnes Scott College. By 1912, twenty-seven houses had been built, six by Mayson and Weekes.[12] The neighborhood now known as the McDonough–Adams St.–King's Highway (MAK) Historic District, which includes the Mayson and Weekes development, was listed on the National Register of Historic Places in 2013, with twenty-one houses designed by Wilburn.[13]

The Mayson and Weekes development would be instrumental in Wilburn's early success in supplying house plans to developers and developing her practice as a plan book architect. Houses on Adams Street are among the earliest residences known to have been designed by the young architect. Many would later be offered as plan designs in Wilburn's first plan book, *Southern Homes and Bungalows*, in 1914, so that additional houses could be built from these plans. They represent significant professional accomplishments that enabled her to launch her plan book business. From the time that Wilburn began her architectural practice, the development of her plan book business was linked to the success of residential builders and developers such as Mayson and Weekes, who used her house plans to build homes in new residential neighborhoods.

At the time of her father's death in 1909, when he was fifty-eight years old, Wilburn shared a home with her mother and younger siblings, Joseph, Ross, Alice, and Llewellyn on N. Candler Street in Decatur, according to 1910 census records. In 1910 Wilburn built her own home in the Mayson and Weekes development, on a residential lot on Adams Street, where she would maintain a residence for the rest of her life. Later that year, the household moved to Wilburn's new home at 127 Adams Street, which Wilburn would share with family members for many years.[14] Except for her three years of service during World War II, Wilburn lived at 127 Adams Street her entire adult life. For more than fifty years she commuted from her Decatur home to her office in downtown Atlanta, which was then about a twenty-minute ride away on the street car and later by bus.

In 1911 Wilburn's sister Alice moved into a house nearby, at 115 Adams Street, and although Alice married and moved to South Carolina shortly afterward, she returned to the house, along with her three young children, when her husband, William Frierson, died in 1918.[15] Alice's daughter, Elizabeth "Lib" Frierson Kennedy, remembered Wilburn as hard-working

and adventurous, but most of all as a kind and generous aunt. Lib recalled growing up down the street and spending afternoons with her, explaining, "Everyone knew her as 'Aunt Lee.'"[16] Aunt Lee could be counted on to remember every birthday and special occasion, especially Christmas. According to Lib, she and her siblings enjoyed visiting Wilburn in her downtown office, which was a particularly good place from which to view local parades.

Wilburn's niece Lib Frierson married Leland Kennedy in 1937, and in 1949 she and her family moved into their new home at 314 Adams Street, where they lived for many years. According to Lib's daughter, Lib often sent her and her siblings down the street to visit and play at Aunt Lee's house on Sunday afternoons, just as her mother, Alice Frierson, had done when Lib was a child.[17] Throughout her adult life, Leila Ross Wilburn remained close to her immediate family as well as her extended family of nieces and nephews. Wilburn's sister, Llewellyn, a professor in the physical education department at Agnes Scott College, lived with Wilburn in the house on Adams Street for some years, and Wilburn had a positive influence on her nephew Joseph Wilburn, the son of her brother Walter Ross, who later became an architect in the Atlanta area.[18]

Leila Ross Wilburn's life ended November 13, 1967, a few days before her eighty-second birthday, in her 127 Adams Street house in Decatur where she had lived for almost sixty years, in a beautiful neighborhood with houses that she had designed, in a community where she was known and appreciated. She was laid to rest next to her parents in the Wilburn family plot in the Decatur Cemetery. Even though Wilburn's accomplishments may not have been fully recognized during her lifetime, recent critical appreciations, such as her 2003 induction into the Georgia Women's Hall of Fame,[19] show that her legacy is beginning to be properly understood, and the houses she designed for several generations serve as an enduring testimony to her achievement.

SOUTHERN HOMES AND PLAN BOOKS

A Man's Profession, a Woman's Domain   *Leila Ross Wilburn's Architectural Practice and Plan Book Business*

WHEN WILBURN OPENED her architectural office in Atlanta in 1908, her first commissions included private residences for clients in the Atlanta area, as well as several apartment buildings. She also designed some commercial and institutional facilities.[1] At the same time, Wilburn began providing residential house plans to builders and developers who were constructing homes in the Atlanta area. Six years later, Wilburn published her first plan book, offering mail-order house plans in a variety of architectural styles. Her ambition to make house designs affordable and readily available throughout the South led her to publish her designs in plan books and to advertise her plan books in newspapers and other publications. In launching her plan book business, Wilburn extended her reach as an architect. She offered mail-order house plans for smaller, well-designed homes for the middle class in plan books that were published from 1914 to 1960. This strategy distinguished her architectural practice and would define her legacy as one of extraordinary achievement and lasting influence. Her plan book designs were used to build houses in newly developed suburbs, small towns, and neighborhoods throughout the Southeast. These plan book houses are particularly prevalent in the Atlanta area, where Wilburn maintained her practice throughout her career.

The first subdivision known to have been developed using a significant number of Wilburn's early plan book designs was in Decatur, Georgia, a historic town six miles east of Atlanta where Wilburn would make her home.[2] As mentioned in the introduction, in 1907 John Mayson and Poleman Weekes bought a large tract of undeveloped land in Decatur south of College Avenue with the intention of converting it into a residential suburb. Located along streetcar lines with close proximity to the Decatur train depot, the courthouse square, the central business district, and Agnes Scott Institute, the land was a particularly attractive location for a new residential suburb. Soon after Wilburn opened

FIGURE I.I. This undated photograph of Leila Ross Wilburn at a train depot is one of a few surviving photographs that document Wilburn's travels as a young architect.

her office, she designed a number of houses that were built by developers Mayson & Weekes in their new subdivision, which is now part of the McDonough–Adams St.–King's Highway (MAK) Historic District. Plans of many of these houses were later offered as mail-order house plans in Wilburn's first plan book, *Southern Homes and Bungalows*, published in 1914.[3] These early plan book houses were designed with architectural features that Wilburn's plan designs would become known for: spacious, light-filled interiors, corner bedrooms, a large porch, and flexible living spaces.

In the introduction to her first plan book, Wilburn stated: "Here will be found plans for moderate-cost residences . . . in selecting the homes for this publication only those of good plan arrangement and sensible construction have been used. . . . In the floor plans, in no case, has the comfort and convenience of the house been sacrificed to make it easier to get the desired exterior effect."[4] As she would in her other plan books, Wilburn offered a variety of house plans that were designed to be economical, modern homes for the growing middle class.

The plan design shown in Figure 1.2, plan no. 655, is a good example of a two-story "southern home" offered in *Southern Homes and Bungalows*. Wilburn described the house in this way: "An eight-room house of simple lines is here shown, but of marked excellence of design, the rounded gabled windows are particularly attractive and the massive porch columns, with ornamental caps are in keeping with the dark stained exterior, and heavy brick foundation."[5] This house, shown in Figure 1.3, was built on Adams Street in the Mayson & Weeks development. With spacious interiors, a simple floor plan, and a large front porch, it was similar in style and interior arrangement to many of Wilburn's southern homes based on the four-square house type. The first level featured typical living spaces, including living, dining, and kitchen areas, and the second floor provided three spacious corner bedrooms, a bath, and sleeping porch. This floor plan offered flexibility in opening up rooms on the first level for

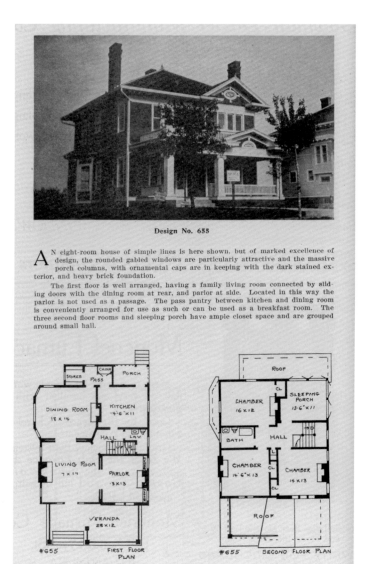

FIGURE 1.2. Plan design no. 655 in *Southern Homes and Bungalows* was a typical southern home design with four spacious rooms on each level and a large veranda across the front of the house.

FIGURE 1.3. This early plan book house was built on Adams Street from
plan design no. 655 in *Southern Homes and Bungalows*.

entertaining. Large windows provided good cross-ventilation, daylight, and exterior views.

Southern Homes and Bungalows included photographs and stock mail-order plans for eighty-two houses in a large, 8-by-11-inch format (see Fig. 1.4). Wilburn called the volume "a collection of choice designs."[6] The photographs included in it likely were of houses that were built during her first five years of architectural practice—an indication of her early success in supplying large numbers of house plans to developers and contractors as a residential architect. Outstanding examples from her first plan book include many homes built on Adams Street in Decatur, a street where Wilburn maintained a residence her entire adult life.

For more than five decades, Wilburn's unique architectural practice and successful plan book business responded to the need for economical, well-designed homes for the middle class. They reflected current trends in the design of the American home and the changing needs of homeowners during successive periods of progressive expansion, economic hardship, wartime shortages, and post-war prosperity. As a plan book architect, she became a strong advocate for prospective homeowners, with a deep commitment to providing attractive and affordable mail-order house designs in a variety of sizes and styles. Wilburn's plan book business allowed her to expand her reach far and wide, offering high-quality, low-cost house plans that made it possible for many throughout the South to build a house they could afford to own.

The colonial revival–style home shown in Figure 1.5 was built on Adams Street from plan design no. 622. It was one of the larger homes offered in Wilburn's first plan book. Plan design no. 842, an early example of one of Wilburn's smaller house designs, was also offered in Wilburn's first plan book. A house was built from this plan in the same neighborhood in Decatur in the early twentieth century, as shown in Figure 1.6.

In supplying mail-order house plans in published plan books, Wilburn's timing couldn't have been better. Atlanta was growing and, like

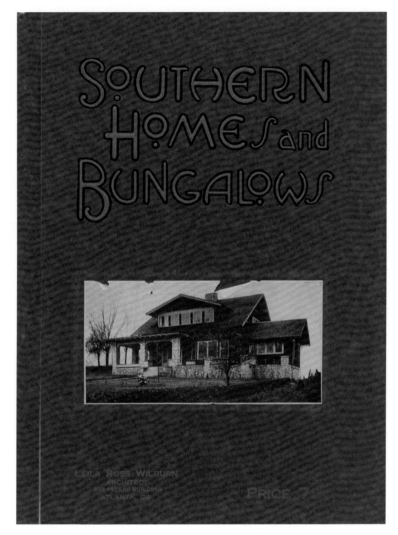

FIGURE 1.4. The front cover of *Southern Homes and Bungalows*, Wilburn's first plan book, shows a house that had been built from one of the plan designs. This plan book was published in 1914 in a large, 8-by-11-inch format and sold for seventy-five cents.

Design No. 842

This two-story residence, though occupying a small amount of ground, has an air of roominess about it. The veranda, with its entrance at one end, leaves the main part so that it can be fitted up as a summer living room. The stairway is cut off from the main living room by French glass doors. This makes the room easier to heat by a fireplace. The second floor has, besides the three bed rooms, a fine sleeping porch.

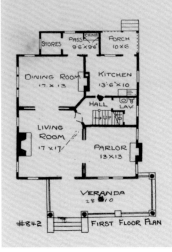

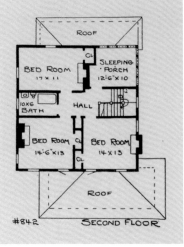

FIGURE 1.5. This two-story colonial revival southern home was built from plan design no. 622 on Adams Street in Decatur, Ga.

FIGURE 1.6. Plan design no. 842, from *Southern Homes and Bungalows*, represents a small two-story house with a large veranda designed to be "fitted up as a summer living room." It included a large sleeping porch on the second level.

many other American cities, was experiencing an acute housing shortage. Residential development was a booming industry, expanding at a rapid pace to provide housing for new residents. Cheap, undeveloped land beyond the commercial downtown area, along with transportation improvements such as expanded streetcar lines, paved roads, and the mass production of the automobile, facilitated the development of suburbs for a growing population. These suburban developments offered residential lots for builders and prospective homeowners in attractive locations that were desirable places to live. Land was plentiful; houses were not.

On a national level, the shortage of housing stock in urban areas attracted attention from the business community as a concern that affected business interests and urban vitality. The "Own Your Own Home" movement, which began before World War I as a U.S. Department of Labor initiative, gained momentum after the war as a national response by realtors, businessmen, and civic leaders to the high cost of rental housing and the national shortage in housing stock.[7] Expositions were held in major cities such as Boston, New York, and San Francisco in an effort to stimulate the home-building industries in these cities. In 1922, the Atlanta Real Estate Board organized the first "Own Your Own Home" building exposition in the South, an initiative led by a committee of the Real Estate Board and organized as a week-long, public event. After months of organizing, the exposition was held in Atlanta, and its success was reported in the organization's 1922 yearbook, with the following description:

> And so the "Own Your Own Home" exposition became a reality. The public is now reaping the benefits of the work, which has been done during the past four months. They may come and see under one roof all the various items which enter into home building, from the proposed site to the final coverage of the completed home with insurance. . . .
>
> Now in the exhibits which have been assembled, practically every dream can be realized. A wide variety of materials and methods are at the

FIGURE 1.7. This advertisement for Leila Ross Wilburn's first two plan books, *Southern Homes and Bungalows* and *Brick and Colonial Homes*, and for Wilburn's booklet "Up-To-Date Homes," was featured in the 1922 yearbook of the Atlanta Real Estate Board.

exposition for consideration. The latest novelties, the newest designs, the most progressive methods are to be seen.

> The Atlanta Real Estate Board hopes that every man and woman who visits the show will carry away something that will aid them in realizing the "dream home"; and if thousands of persons are led to begin building their own homes as a result of the displays . . . then all the labor which has gone towards assembling the displays will have been well worth while.[8]

When the 1922 "Own Your Own Home" building exposition was held in Atlanta, Wilburn had just published her second plan book, *Brick and Colonial Homes*, and she participated in the exposition.[9] The Atlanta Real Estate Board's 1922 yearbook included "plans, suggestions, and advice for home builders" as well as advertisements for many businesses associated with the home building industry.[10] It also featured twenty-three stock plans and two pages of advertisements from Wilburn's second plan book, a clear indication of the strong support for Wilburn's plan book business in the real estate profession (see Fig. 1.7).[11]

Interestingly, the Wilburn mail-order house plans that were offered in the yearbook included the cost of construction of each house design. This information would have helped prospective homeowners in the Atlanta area in choosing a house design that they could afford. The cost of construction was not provided in any of Wilburn's published plan books, since the mail-order plans were meant for regional distribution and construction costs could vary depending on local conditions, particularly labor and material costs.[12]

The craftsman bungalow featured in the advertisement shown in Figure 1.7 also was included on a separate page as a mail-order plan in the 1922 yearbook, as shown in Figure 1.8. This listing did provide the cost of construction: $4,750 for the design in frame (wood) and $5,500 for the house built with a stucco exterior. A house built on North Highland Avenue in Atlanta from this plan, plan design no. 138, is shown in Figure 1.9.

Although Wilburn maintained an architectural office in downtown Atlanta, many of her early residential designs were built in neighborhoods

FIGURE 1.8. This advertisement for plan design no. 138 was published in the 1922 yearbook of the Atlanta Real Estate Board. Houses were built using this design in several Atlanta neighborhoods, including Lake Claire, Morningside, and Virginia-Highland.

FIGURE 1.9. This house on North Highland Avenue in the Virginia-Highland neighborhood in Atlanta is a beautiful example of a house built from plan design no. 138, which was published in Wilburn's second plan book, *Brick and Colonial Homes*, as well as in the Atlanta Real Estate Board's 1922 Year Book.

and streetcar suburbs in Decatur neighborhoods such as the Mayson & Weekes subdivision and Ponce de Leon Terrace. As her plan book business grew, contractors, developers, and homeowners purchased Wilburn's stock, mail-order house plans for Atlanta's garden suburbs and neighborhoods, including Ansley Park, Candler Park, Druid Hills, Inman Park, Lake Claire, Midtown, Morningside, and Virginia-Highland. As new Atlanta suburbs were developed through the 1960s, Wilburn's plan books continued to offer a variety of economical house plans in popular architectural styles.

Wilburn described another of her early plan designs, plan design no. 764, shown in Figure 1.10, as follows: "Beam ceilings, panel work and plate rails give an artistic touch to the interior. The breakfast room and lavatory are added conveniences on the first floor. The second story has a compact hall from which the four bed rooms and bath are entered. Closets to each room, linen closet and sleeping porch make this floor complete. Furnace heat in the basement is provided."[13] Her plan book houses typically included an abundance of storage spaces, flexible living spaces, and large porches designed as outdoor living rooms. The rooms in this plan were spacious, and, as in many of Wilburn's designs, the first-floor plan was arranged so that living spaces (living, dining, parlor, library, den spaces) could be used separately or opened up as one large gathering space for entertaining. These features and would become trademarks of Wilburn's designs, offering flexibility, efficiency, and practicality in function and arrangement. A house from this plan design was built on Adams Street in Decatur, as shown in Figure 1.11.

Wilburn's upbringing in a southern, middle-class family that valued education likely instilled in her a sense of vocation and a desire for professional achievement. With her family's support, Wilburn became a talented architect and a savvy businesswoman, succeeding in a time, a place, and a profession in which few individuals would have expected a woman to have much influence. Although the specific challenges she encountered

Design No. 764

I N this dignified home the granite piers and balustrade present a strong and durable front, while the fluted columns with ornamental caps lighten the design.

The entrance hall contains a well planned stairway and this room together with the living and dining rooms open up so that the first floor can be thrown into practically one large room. Beam ceilings, panel work and plate rails give an artistic touch to the interior. The breakfast room and lavatory are added conveniences on the first floor. The second story has a compact hall from which the four bed rooms and bath are entered. Closets to each room, linen closet and sleeping porch make this floor complete. Furnace heat in the basement is provided. The first story height is ten feet and the second nine feet.

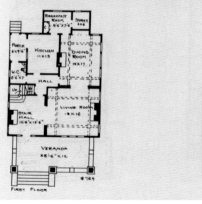

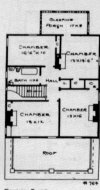

FIGURE 1.10. The exterior photograph of plan design no. 764 in *Southern Homes and Bungalows* appears to have been taken just after the house was constructed on undeveloped property.

FIGURE I.II. This historic home, built from plan design no. 764 on Adams Street in Decatur, Ga., has been preserved with its original exterior features. The front porch has been screened to provide a more functional outdoor living area.

as a woman in the male-dominated profession of architecture are not known, Wilburn's success seems to have hinged on her ability to turn professional obstacles into opportunities that supported her career ambitions. First and perhaps foremost, she charted a different course from the traditional career path of an architect, beginning with her education and training. After attending Agnes Scott Institute in Decatur, Wilburn began working at B. R. Padgett & Sons, an Atlanta architectural and construction firm, instead of enrolling in a university to study architecture. After working for two years as an apprentice and a draftsperson in the firm, Wilburn opened her office in downtown Atlanta, with commercial as well as residential clients in her first years of practice. She soon began

publishing plan books, supplying contractors, developers, and homeowners with stock house plans for well-designed economical homes. Although little is known about the size of her office or its operations, records indicate that she employed four draftsmen during most of her years of practice.[14]

Rather than working directly with individual clients to provide residential design services, Wilburn's plan book business focused on the products of architectural services—that is, supplying the drawings and specifications needed by a contractor to build the house. Although Wilburn provided some traditional architectural design services for custom commissions, she had the strongest influence in shaping residential development through her plan book business.

Most significantly, Wilburn was not just in the business of selling plans—she was selling good designs and offering variety, affordability, and convenience in the delivery of architectural plans and specifications that were ready to purchase. Her plan book houses were what she advocated for in her second plan book: "a better class of small domestic architecture."[15] They were high-quality designs, beautiful and well-crafted, as well as efficient, economical, and practical for a diverse clientele. And, as Wilburn explained, they were designed with the same level of attention and thoughtfulness as a custom designed home, at a fraction of the cost (as a mail-order stock plan).[16]

When Wilburn began her career in the early twentieth century, architecture was a profession that few women chose. The home, however, was traditionally considered a woman's domain, with women assuming the typical responsibilities of household organization, upkeep, furnishings, and domestic work in support of family life. In her plan books, Wilburn marketed herself as an architect with special expertise in designing domestic space because she was a woman. She explicitly reinforced the idea of the home as a woman's area of expertise, writing, for example, "I feel that, being a woman, I know just the little things that should go in a house to make living in it a pleasure to the entire family."[17]

In designing domestic space, Wilburn created interiors that reflected current trends and included popular features in the design of the modern American home. In the early decades of the twentieth century, popular features included built-in furnishings that offered efficient storage and flexible living spaces. Bookcases, window seats, buffets, concealed beds, and even ironing boards were among the built-in furnishings in Wilburn's early house plans. They reflected Wilburn's careful attention to detail in creating compact floor plans and flexible living spaces for economical, modern homes for the middle class. Wilburn also designed spaces for laundry facilities, sewing machines, heating systems, and other household improvements, which increased the efficiency, comfort, and functionality of her

plan book houses overall. In addition, Wilburn typically included generous amounts of storage space, including kitchen pantries, linen closets, trunk rooms, and utility closets—support spaces that added functionality and convenience to her plan book houses. In later plan books, Wilburn offered smaller homes with more compact floor plans that included open living spaces, family rooms, eat-in kitchens, and attached garages, reflecting the changing needs and current trends in residential design.

Wilburn's education as an architect followed a traditional path of training and apprenticeship rather than a formal architectural education. At the turn of the century, there were few architectural schools in the United States, and almost all of them were located in the Northeast. For women interested in an architectural education, the limitations were even greater, with few schools allowing women to enroll.[18] At the time, however, an alternative to a formal architectural education (for both men and women) was to acquire skills and training through a paid apprenticeship. An apprentice would learn architectural drafting, design, and construction through direct experience, working for an architect or construction professional and eventually acquiring the necessary knowledge and experience to work independently as an architect.[19] It is not known whether Wilburn ever applied to or considered enrolling in an architecture school to obtain a formal architectural education.

According to a family member, Wilburn took private architectural drafting lessons as a young woman and learned how to produce architectural drawings, after expressing an interest to her parents in acquiring these skills.[20] As mentioned previously, soon after she completed her studies at Agnes Scott Institute (1902–1904), Wilburn worked as a draftsperson with an established architectural design and construction company, B. R. Padgett & Sons, Architects and General Contractors, in Atlanta from 1906 to 1908.[21] An ad for the firm stated: "We prepare plans, make full specifications and estimate cost on all kinds of buildings. Fine residences a specialty."[22] Wilburn may have chosen this path to architecture intentionally, training with architects and builders to gain practical knowledge and experience instead of enrolling in a school of architecture. At B. R. Padgett & Sons, in addition to gaining specific skills and experience in drafting, architectural design, and specifications, Wilburn likely made important connections with residential building trades, suppliers, developers, and contractors in the Atlanta area.

Although architecture was regarded as a man's profession and was a challenging career path for women, Wilburn was not the only woman in the profession in Georgia in the early twentieth century. Henrietta Dozier (1872–1947), who graduated from the Massachusetts Institute of Technology in 1899, became one of the first women to practice architecture in Georgia and had established a successful business by the time Wilburn began her career. Dozier worked in the Atlanta area until 1916, when she moved to Florida and continued her career there. She became the third woman, and the first southern woman, to be admitted as a member of the American Institute of Architects (AIA) in 1905.[23]

A prominent architect in Georgia who was a contemporary of Wilburn, Ellamae Ellis League (1899–1991), from Macon, Georgia, received her architectural education through correspondence courses from the Beaux Arts Institute of Design in New York from 1923 to 1927 and took courses in architecture at the École des Beaux Arts in Fontainebleau, France, from 1927 to 1928. When she returned to Macon, she worked in the office of William Franklin Oliphant until Oliphant's death in 1934. At that time, she became a registered architect in Georgia and opened her own architectural office, taking some commissions from Oliphant's office and practicing architecture until her retirement in 1975.[24] League was an active member of the Atlanta chapter of the AIA and became a fellow in 1968, joining an elite group of architects who had attained this prestigious recognition from the institute.[25]

Ellamae Ellis League's daughter, Jean League Newton, AIA (1919–2000), also became a notable Georgia architect. As a student at Radcliffe in the late 1930s, Jean League Newton, took courses at the Cambridge School for Architecture and Landscape Architecture, the only architecture school founded exclusively for women.[26] After she graduated in 1941, she enrolled in the Cambridge School to study architecture. When the school merged with the Harvard Graduate School of Design the following year, Newton became one of the first women to study at and graduate from Harvard with an architectural degree.[27] In 1944, after graduation, she joined her mother's architectural practice—Ellamae Ellis League, AIA Architect—in Macon and practiced with her for more than thirty years.[28] The prominent architectural firm was known for its outstanding designs, which included commercial, institutional, and public buildings, as well as a number of fine residences in Georgia.[29]

Wilburn opened her own architectural firm in the Peters Building in downtown Atlanta in 1908. As mentioned previously, residential development in Atlanta was booming at this time, and there was a widespread need for housing driven largely by a tremendous population increase that had begun in the late nineteenth century with the city's growth and development. The largest volume of housing demand was driven by the growing middle class, which typically relied on builders rather than architects for house plans.[30]

In developing her plan book business, Wilburn was able to respond directly to the acute need for a large supply of affordable, well-designed house plans in a way that traditional architects were not. Her mail-order house plans were sold at a fraction of the cost of a custom-designed home, and her plan books offered builders and homeowners a wide range of choices in sizes, styles, and plan arrangements. In publishing plan books that were sold to homeowners and builders throughout the South, Wilburn was able to fulfill her ambition to supply southerners near and far with a variety of economical house plans from which to choose a suitable home.

In so doing, she became part of an American plan book tradition that dated back to the nineteenth century. Daniel D. Reiff, in *Houses from*

Books, has documented more than seventy-five companies that published "house-plan books and catalogs" between 1883 and 1951, and more than twenty-five entities that published plan books.[31] In *Texas Houses Built by the Book* (1999), Margaret Culbertson also examined the plan book tradition in the development of American towns and cities, providing a number of examples of Texas houses built from designs in plan books, or mail-order house catalogues.[32]

The American plan book tradition of the twentieth century had its origins in the nineteenth-century pattern books produced as references or guides for residential design and construction. Pattern books typically provided a front elevation or rendering with a floor plan, and they often included architectural details and narratives describing particular architectural features. The primary distinction between nineteenth-century pattern books and the popular plan books that followed some years later was that pattern books offered drawings and specifications for construction as "patterns." Plan books offered either house plans or pre-cut houses for sale by mail order. As Jan Jennings explained, "Although pattern books varied in size and number of designs, all of them offered a full set of scale drawings—a floor plan, elevations, sections, full detail drawings, examples of specifications—and estimates for building materials."[33] By the early twentieth century, mail-order house plans were available for purchase from plan books as well as popular magazines and journals. These stock plans were popular among builders and homeowners and were widely used for construction of new homes throughout the United States.[34] They provided an efficient and economical means for addressing the large-scale demand for housing, particularly in the first decades of the twentieth century, when population growth and economic prosperity supported suburban growth and development.

Although not many architects are known to have published plan books, two notable plan book architects—George Barber and Emily Elizabeth Housman—had produced some important examples by the time Wilburn began her practice.[35] George Barber was a successful, self-trained architect in Knoxville, Tennessee, who published his first plan book in 1887 and his last in 1907. (Barber died in 1915.) His plan books offered a variety of styles, with late-Victorian style houses, particularly those with Queen Anne features, as the most predominant. His firm produced hundreds of designs in a twenty-year span and "probably sold more than twenty thousand sets of plans."[36] Emily Elizabeth Holman, a contemporary of George Barber, also established a successful plan-book business. Unlike Wilburn, who used her full name, Holman used her initials in the name of her architectural practice, E. E. Holman Co., Architects, which concealed her gender. Holman practiced from 1893 to 1914 in Philadelphia and published several plan books, advertising them in popular magazines, including *Ladies Home Journal.*[37]

The tradition of offering mail-order plans in published books appears to have been more common among companies and architectural firms than among individual architects. Beginning in the late nineteenth century, Palliser and Palliser, an architectural firm in Connecticut, published more than twenty such books and became one of the earliest and most successful companies working in this tradition.[38] *The Craftsman*, a magazine published by Gustav Stickley from 1901 to 1916, was a popular source for mail-order house plans for craftsman-style homes, including bungalows, in the arts and crafts tradition. *Ladies Home Journal* and *House Beautiful*, two women's magazines with wide readership and distribution, also offered stock house plans that could be purchased through the mail.[39] The demand for economical house designs was significant, with many sources providing mail-order designs, particularly in the first decades of the twentieth century.

Some companies published ready-cut house catalogues, offering essentially mail-order houses that were shipped throughout the country.[40] These companies were an additional, important part of the plan book tradition. According to Schweitzer and Davis, "There were a 'Big Six' of Midwestern suppliers of pre-cut conventional balloon-frame houses, advertised and sold nationally over several decades: Gordon-Van Tine, Aladdin, Sears, Ward, Lewis, and Sterling."[41] They were large-scale suppliers of prefabricated houses throughout the United States, and they competed with local lumber companies and building trades in supplying materials and labor for the housing industry.

As a young plan book architect, Wilburn embraced her vocation with an eagerness to learn and a determination to succeed. In 1924, fifteen years after she opened her architectural firm, Wilburn was featured in an newspaper article titled "Atlanta Women Have Man-Size Jobs" in the *Atlanta Journal*. In it Wilburn stated, "Many years preparation are required to become an architect. . . . Then, after studying architecture, the beginner's pay is poor. . . . It took me long years to build up a clientele, and I know that the first years are far from easy. This experience is compensated for today, however, by the pleasure which comes from building homes. There is nothing I like better, and I don't believe I'd be satisfied with any other job in the world."[42]

In her third plan book, *Ideal Homes of Today*, Wilburn elaborated on her sources of inspiration, architectural references, and house designs, stating: "I have bought every magazine and plan book I could hear of, therefore I feel that I am able to give you an interesting selection of ideal home designs for the present day."[43] She also educated herself through observation and direct experience—traveling, sketching, reading, recording, photographing—activities that have long been understood as some of the best ways to learn architectural design, historical styles, and building traditions. Indeed, Wilburn traveled extensively and understood travel to be essential to her own professional education and growth as an architect. As she explained in her second plan book, *Brick and Colonial Homes*, in 1921: "For the past fifteen years I have spent my vacations visiting other cities, have taken over 5,000 kodak pictures, made sketches and bought books

so as to keep myself well posted on every new feature in home architecture."[44] Few of these photographs survive, but two of them document trips to North Carolina and Washington, D.C., as shown in Figures 1.12 and 1.13.

FIGURE 1.12. This undated photograph of Leila Ross Wilburn at the Georgia–North Carolina state line may have been taken on one of her many trips to study the architecture of other places, as she stated in her plan books.

FIGURE 1.13. This undated photograph of Leila Ross Wilburn with her sister, Alice Frierson, was taken in Washington, D.C.

There is little surviving information about the reference books Wilburn used or the magazines and journals she read to learn about residential architecture. However, her plan book writings show that she was committed to educating herself about the latest trends and styles in domestic architecture.

As a businesswoman and entrepreneur, Wilburn recognized the importance of advertising her plan books in newspapers and other publications, such as the *Industrial Index*. These ads supported regional distribution of her plan books, making her stock plans more accessible to homebuilders throughout the Southeast. In an advertisement for *Southern Homes and Bungalows* that appeared in the *Industrial Index* in 1914, Wilburn stated

that she had designed more than twelve hundred southern homes, confirming the distinct focus of her practice in supplying stock house plans rather than designing custom houses for individual clients.[45]

In the same way that Wilburn advertised her plan books in newspapers throughout the South, those in the housing industry also advertised their residential products and services. These companies included contractors, building trades, and suppliers of furnishings, systems, and fixtures, as well as banks and realtors. Wilburn's first plan book contained a number of advertisements from local companies in the Atlanta area, and it is the only Wilburn plan book that included advertisements, such as those shown in Figures 1.14 and 1.15.

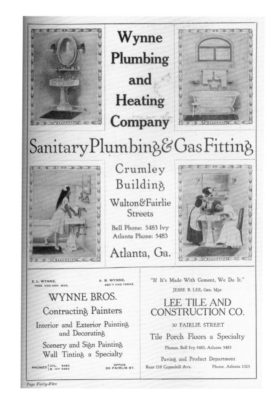

FIGURE 1.14. These advertisements in *Southern Homes and Bungalows* promoted businesses supplying builders with residential materials and heating systems.

FIGURE 1.15. These advertisements in *Southern Homes and Bungalows* marketed the services of modern plumbing and heating system companies, as well as those of painting and tile subcontractors.

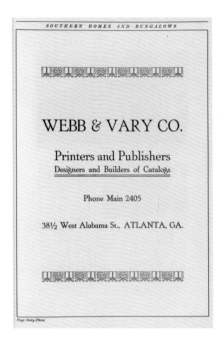

FIGURE 1.16. *Southern Homes and Bungalows* also advertised the services of Webb & Vary Company, a printing and publishing business in Atlanta.

Another advertisement from *Southern Homes and Bungalows* is shown in Figure 1.16, for Webb & Vary Co., who marketed themselves as "Printers and Publishers, Designers and Builders of Catalogs." Although it is not known if this company produced the plan book for Wilburn, it did offer printing and publishing services, and designing and producing catalogs in particular.

In 1917, soon after Wilburn published her first plan book, she put her architectural practice on hold in order to join the Army civilian service during World War I.[46] She served at Fort McPherson in East Point, Georgia, as a draftsperson. After the war, in 1918, Wilburn resumed her architectural practice in the Peters Building in Atlanta.[47] In 1920, when the state of Georgia required architects to become registered, Wilburn met the qualifications and became the 29th of 118 architects and one of two women registered that year.[48] Figure 1.17 shows her architectural registration.

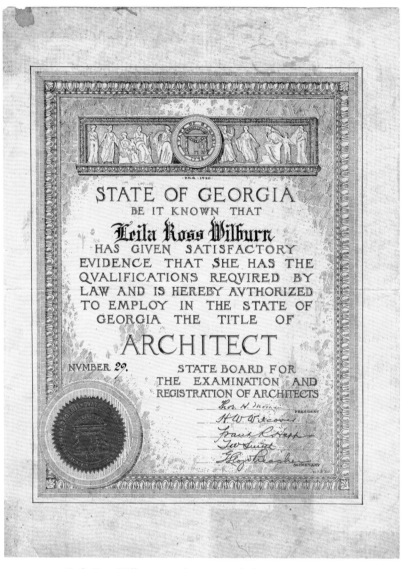

FIGURE 1.17. Leila Ross Wilburn was the twenty-ninth architect registered in Georgia in 1920, the first year that registration for architects was required in the state.

The following year, Wilburn published her second plan book, *Brick and Colonial Homes* (see Fig. 1.18). The volume was a large-format plan book with eighty-six mail-order plan designs. It sold for $2.00.[49] The date of publication was provided in an advertisement for the plan book appearing in the *Atlanta Constitution* on October 30, 1921, that read as follows: "Send for the Newest Plan-Book. 'BRICK AND COLONIAL HOMES'. . . Size 8 x 11 inches. Book shows 86 photos, plans and descriptions. Plans are ready to mail out on receipt of order. The book contains plans ranging in price from economical five-room houses to the more elaborate designs of one and two stories."[50]

In *Brick and Colonial Homes*, Wilburn provided detailed information about the cost for stock plans, about what the plans included, about her own business practices and policies, and ordering information.[51] In the foreword, Wilburn offered a more comprehensive description of her plan book business than those found in subsequent plan books. She also explained the characteristics of materials and advised homeowners to select the exterior material for their home carefully, with a clear understanding of the advantages of each material. In describing brick as a choice for the exterior façade, Wilburn wrote:

> There is nothing which will give the house so much dignity, stability and permanence as brick. To some of us brick means the old style common brick, while to others of us it stands for a building material that only the richest can afford. The extra cost for veneering a house with face brick is very little when one takes into consideration that with brick outside walls the insurance rate is lower; the house is cooler in summer and warmer in winter; and the cost of upkeep is materially reduced. Now that the newer tapestry brick can be had in such rich and varied finishes and colorings, some most pleasing exteriors are now obtained in brick homes.[52]

A large two-story brick home, plan design no. 1005, was featured on the first page of Wilburn's next plan book, *Ideal Homes of Today*, as shown in

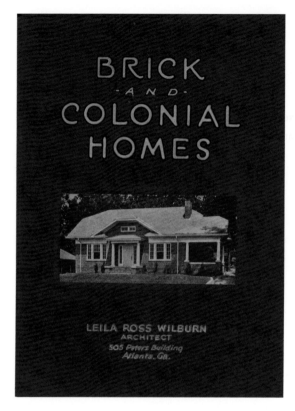

FIGURE 1.18. The front cover of *Brick and Colonial Homes*, Wilburn's second plan book, included her office address and a photograph of one of her plan book houses. It was published in 1921 and contained eighty-six plan designs. This plan book sold for two dollars.

Figure 1.19. Brick was a popular and economical choice in Georgia, as a building material that was manufactured and distributed in the state. An advertisement for Legg Brick Company, a Georgia brick company with Atlanta offices, was included in Wilburn's first plan book, as shown in Figure 1.20.

However, for the popular colonial revival style and for a more economical exterior of any style home, Wilburn considered a wood frame exterior to be an excellent choice (see Fig. 1.5 earlier in the chapter for a house with such an exterior). She explained:

The frame house needs no introduction, it is suitable for many localities, can be made most attractive, and on account of the low cost is one of the most popular materials of which to build. It is only in comparatively recent years that the more discerning public has turned with appreciation and respect to the beauty of the early Colonial traditions. In the new Colonial homes boxed eaves are used as well as the ones with exposed rafter ends, the stoop at the entrance gives access to the house so that the side porch, now so often seen, may be private. Homes of this design, although not always purely Colonial, show a touch of that type here and there, which, added to the general simplicity of the design, makes a home that is not only distinctive, but one that will withstand the critical test of time.[53]

For colonial, Spanish, and Italian revival style homes in particular, and as a material to use in gable ends of brick exterior houses, Wilburn recommended stucco as an exterior finish:

A well built stucco house is attractive, it is lasting, comfortable and its cost is not prohibitive. The "up-keep" is less than the weather-boarded house and although it need never be painted its color can be changed by the use of specially prepared paints. In brick houses stucco is much in demand for use in the gable ends. Colonial, Spanish and Italian designs can be well carried out where stucco is used for exterior finish.[54]

An attractive stucco plan book design is shown in Figure 1.20.

In her next plan book, *Ideal Homes of Today*, Wilburn continued to encourage homeowners to consider the exterior appearance of their houses in the context of their neighborhoods, explaining: "We owe something to our neighbors; we do care what they think of the appearance of our home." She then defined her idea of the "ideal home" as "a well-balanced structure, harmonious in detail, and attractive outside as well as inside."[55]

At the bottom of each page in *Brick and Colonial Homes* and *Ideal Homes of Today*, Wilburn's second and third plan books, she offered a "building idea" as a design tip on a variety of house-related topics. The

FIGURE 1.19. The first page of *Ideal Homes of Today* was dedicated to a large southern home with more than 3,200 square feet on two levels. It features a front terrace and side porch with a first-level floor plan that Wilburn described as "unusual and well adapted for entertaining." The second-level corner bedrooms were "exceptionally large," with direct connections to baths and closets. The second level also included a large sleeping porch.

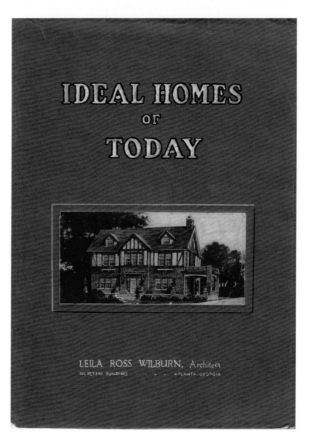

FIGURE 1.20. The advertisement for Legg Brick Company, a local Atlanta brick company, was published on page 89 in *Southern Homes and Bungalows* with plan design no. 538 for a house with a stucco exterior.

She also advocated for well-designed plans in her building tips, stating, "Well designed plans make a well-built house worth its cost."[57]

Wilburn's third plan book, *Ideal Homes of Today*, was published ca. 1925 (see Fig. 1.21). It offered a hundred house designs, and Wilburn stated that "in each is combined artistic beauty in appearance, convenience, and utility in arrangement, and practical economy in construction."[58] The designs

tips range from site selection and neighborhood context to interior finishes and served as advice and counsel to prospective homeowners. Some examples are listed below:

"The plans here offered are revelations in the utilization of space."

"In selecting materials the 'up-keep' should be considered."

"Use plenty of windows, sunlight is cheaper than doctor's bills."

"My plans are practical, therefore they save you money."

"A good home is a debt every man owes his wife."

"A man's character is shown in his home."

"Have the wife's workshop complete—it improves the cooking."[56]

FIGURE 1.21. The front cover of *Ideal Homes of Today*, Wilburn's third plan book, included her office address and a rendering of one of her plan designs. This plan book offered a hundred plan designs and sold for two dollars.

were published in a large, 8-by-11-inch plan book format, as with her previous plan books. It offered similar architectural styles to those published in her second plan book, which included predominantly bungalows and period houses, as well as colonial revival homes.

In *Ideal Homes of Today*, Wilburn explained the difference between a custom-designed plan and a mail-order plan ready for purchase. She advised homeowners to choose the plan that they considered to be the most suitable and to have a contractor make any minor changes, which would be much more economical than requesting a custom design. Custom designs were approximately four times the cost of a stock plan, as Wilburn explained: "Sometimes slight changes are desired. If you have a good contractor the changes may be marked on the blueprint and you can use the stock plan. However, if the changes wanted are extensive, complicated or you want something entirely different it will be necessary to have new plans drawn. Absolutely no changes will be made on the stock plans; do not ask it."[59]

Another business practice that supported Wilburn's goal of providing affordable houses was her exchange policy on stock plans. In her first plan book, she stated that she would provide an estimate of the cost of construction, based on the cost of the house where it was originally built. In later plan books she advised clients to purchase the plan design they liked most. She agreed to exchange their purchased drawings for a design that cost less if their contractor's estimate for the desired plan design was more than they could afford.

In several of her later plan books, Wilburn emphasized the importance of having well-designed house plans. In *Homes in Good Taste*, her fourth plan book, Wilburn described the "Advantages of a Good Plan" as follows:

The economy, convenience, and appearance of a house are largely dependent upon the care and thought that has been employed in designing it. Architects get more rooms out of the allotted space; the plans "work out,"

there is room for stairs, the second story fits over the first story; furniture space and closets are provided; you know beforehand how the house will look; you are protected in case of disagreements; building laws are followed; windows and doors are placed and are of the correct size in relate to the wall space so as to give you a well designed home and the most for your money.[60]

Wilburn knew that good design required not only knowledge of construction materials, methods, systems, and building components but also an understanding of scale, proportion, and balance to achieve a beautiful, harmonious design. Drawings that fully described the size, arrangement, and characteristics of a space provided the contractor with all the information needed to build the space according to plans and specifications.

In most of her plan books, Wilburn explained her business practices and what a mail-order set of complete "plans and specifications" included. For example, in *Ideal Homes of Today*, she wrote, "The plans are practical working drawings, made to a scale of one-fourth inch to the foot and furnished in blueprint form. They cover foundation, floor and roof plans, exterior elevations (and to a larger scale) details of exterior millwork and interior built-in features. The specifications are particularly prepared for each house, supplement the drawings, and cover masonry, plastering, carpentry, hardware, electric work, screens, plumbing, heating, metal work, painting, etc."[61] She also emphasized the reliability and originality of her designs, reassuring homeowners and contractors that she had designed each house and that houses had been built successfully from the house plans: "The plans shown in this book are my personal designs; they are not photographs of other architect's work. Many of the houses have been built several times and builders will find that they 'work out' correctly. All room sizes show inside measurements."[62]

For an additional cost, Wilburn provided a lumber and mill list, which gave "the size, length and number of pieces of all framing, also the size and quantity of all mill work such as doors, windows, flooring, laths, built-in features." This list would have been extremely helpful for contractors to use in ordering pre-cut lumber, standard building materials, and building components, rather than having to develop their own building supply list and calculate the size and quantity of materials needed for construction. A "reverse plan" could be purchased at the same cost as the one published in the plan book. As Wilburn explained, "everything is reversed, plans are redrawn so that lettering reads correctly. Note this when looking over the designs as sometimes the reversed plan will 'be just what you want' when the plan as shown would not do at all."[63]

Typically, each stock plan ordered from a plan book included an exterior rendering or a photograph of the front of the house, the floor plans for each level, and the square footage of each floor, as well as porches, terraces, and outdoor spaces. For each plan design, Wilburn provided a full description of the features of each house and of how rooms might be used. She assigned a plan number to each stock plan, with the cost for plans and specifications, extra sets, and a lumber and mill list. She often included two or three stock plans on one page. Some house designs featured an exterior rendering with several floor plans to choose from.

In later plan books, Wilburn often provided a list of previous plan books, which were available for purchase. For example, in *Ranch and Colonial Homes* (her eighth plan book), she wrote: "Select the design that will best fit your needs. The group of attractive and practical homes illustrated in this book was especially designed for the average American family. If you do not find the house to suit your desires in 'Ranch and Colonial Homes,' see page 56 for a list of my previous plan-books. The designs shown in one plan-book are not repeated in any other book."[64]

Wilburn's first three plan books were similar in design and page layout, with a large, 8-by-11-inch format. In these plan books, each plan design included floor plans, a front elevation or view, and a narrative describing the design features, as well as the cost of the "complete plans and specifications," "extra sets," and a "lumber and mill list." These plan books all offered a diverse collection of floor plans and architectural styles, ranging from bungalows to period homes, European-inspired period houses, English vernacular cottages, and ranch houses. Each plan book contained approximately fifty to one hundred house designs from which stock plans and specifications could be ordered. A set of drawings ranged in price from fifteen to forty dollars per set, and, for an additional cost, usually five dollars, Wilburn would provide a complete lumber and millwork list.

Most of Wilburn's later plan books, including *New Homes of Quality*, *Small Low-Cost Homes for the South*, *Sixty Good New Homes*, and *Ranch and Colonial Homes*, were smaller publications both in trim size and in the number of designs offered.

While the plan book business in general declined significantly around 1940, with many companies going out of business, Wilburn continued to publish plan books and practice architecture until her death in 1967.[65] In addition to her nine large plan books, Wilburn also published smaller booklets as offprints of the previously published books. These booklets containing previously published house plans were created primarily for builders. *One-Story Houses* was a fifteen-page booklet with fourteen designs selected from her second and third plan books for builders. She offered an order of 100 booklets for $5.00 with "Your name printed on both Booklet and Envelope to fit," or "$4.00 per 100 postpaid Booklet only—no Printing," for builders and developers to offer to prospective clients. In *One-Story Houses* she wrote: "In this booklet I am showing a few of the one story houses, selected from the large books. Many builders need such a booklet as it keeps the prospective client from being confused by the more expensive designs."[66] *New Plans for Home Builders* was a later booklet with eighteen house designs selected from her fourth plan book, *Homes in Good Taste*.

Wilburn's desire to design houses for the middle class—for individuals who could afford to own their own homes but who weren't wealthy—led her to develop a successful and long-lasting plan book business. She claimed her expertise as a woman and demonstrated her knowledge of domestic space through her house designs. Instead of competing with other architects for individual clients and custom commissions, Wilburn aligned herself with residential contractors, developers, and middle-class homeowners. Publishing plan books allowed her to offer residential house plans, which were designed to be functionally innovative, economically affordable, and regionally available as low-cost, mail-order house plans. Her plan book publishing business also fulfilled her desire to provide small towns and rural communities with greater access to affordable, well-designed houses.[67]

Given Wilburn's expressed interest in providing affordable house plans to homeowners throughout the South, she seems to have considered her plan book business to be a vocation worthy of her dedication throughout her career. There is no evidence that she considered her plan book practice a limitation or as inferior in any way to a traditional architectural practice. Rather, she seemingly chose it as a preferred path in order to have a greater influence in making high-quality, economical house plans widely available throughout the region.

Wilburn's plan book business outlasted many of the early twentieth-century companies that offered mail-order house plans, as well as those offering pre-cut, mail-order houses. Wilburn published her last plan book, *Bran-New Homes*, in 1960 at the age of seventy-five. Just before this ninth plan book was published, she received a letter from a prospective homeowner in Alabama who described the type of house she was looking for

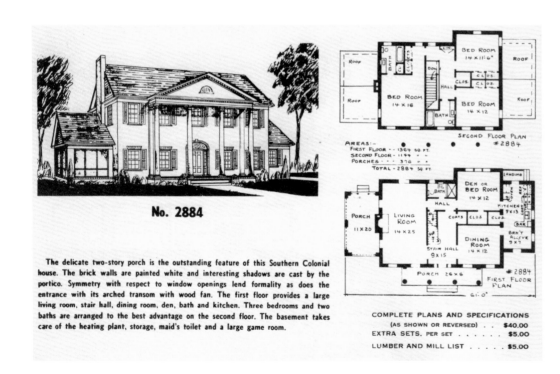

No. 2884

The delicate two-story porch is the outstanding feature of this Southern Colonial house. The brick walls are painted white and interesting shadows are cast by the portico. Symmetry with respect to window openings lend formality as does the entrance with its arched transom with wood fan. The first floor provides a large living room, stair hall, dining room, den, bath and kitchen. Three bedrooms and two baths are arranged to the best advantage on the second floor. The basement takes care of the heating plant, storage, maid's toilet and a large game room.

COMPLETE PLANS AND SPECIFICATIONS
(AS SHOWN OR REVERSED) . . $40.00
EXTRA SETS, PER SET $5.00
LUMBER AND MILL LIST $5.00

FIGURE 1.22. Plan design no. 2884 was offered in *Bran-New Homes*, Wilburn's ninth and last plan book, which was published in 1960.

and had not found in *Ranch and Colonial Homes* (Wilburn's eighth plan book). In keeping with her business practice of trying to find a suitable stock plan for homeowners who sent her design requests, Wilburn replied and sent another plan design, explaining that she intended to publish the plan, no. 2884, a plan design for a two-story southern colonial home, in her next plan book. The client wrote back and said that the plan was "exactly right" and inquired about when she could purchase the plan.[68] This stock plan for a two-story colonial revival home was published in Wilburn's last plan book, *Bran-New Homes*, in 1960 (see Fig. 1.22).

There are no records to indicate how many copies of each plan book were printed and sold throughout Wilburn's career or exactly who bought them. The total number of houses built from Wilburn's stock plans, their geographical locations, and how many are still enjoyed as residences is a matter of speculation, as well as an opportunity for further research. However, records do indicate that she advertised in several southern cities, and Wilburn's houses have been documented in seven states. This evidence suggests that there are many unidentified houses that were built from mail-order house plans that had been selected and ordered from one of Wilburn's plan books.[69]

As a plan book architect, Wilburn transcended limitations of education and gender, turning what were seemingly obstacles into opportunities that supported her professional ambition. In doing so, she created a unique place for herself in the profession and became an influential architect in Georgia in the first half of the twentieth century. Wilburn's plan book houses contribute to the character, scale, and charm of towns throughout the South and are recognized as some of the most attractive and desirable homes in historic neighborhoods throughout the Atlanta area. Her success as a plan book architect can be measured at least in part by the hundreds of known houses she designed, by the number of plan books she published, and by her decades of contributing to the development of twentieth-century suburbs, particularly in Georgia. These indicators show that Wilburn's plan book business and architectural practice were not only successful but also wildly influential, leaving behind an impressive legacy of beautifully designed houses with enduring value and wide appeal.

CHAPTER 2

Southern Comfort, American Style *Leila Ross Wilburn's Early Plan Book Houses*

AS DISCUSSED IN CHAPTER 1, Leila Ross Wilburn realized her ambition to supply house designs to builders and homeowners throughout the Southeast by developing a successful plan book business that lasted from 1914 to 1967. When she began her architectural practice, there was an acute need for more affordable houses for the middle class, particularly in growing urban areas such as Atlanta. This need increased the demand for simple and smaller house designs that reflected new priorities in designs for the American home. Wilburn's response was to supply more economical house designs, offering a variety of mail-order floor plans in a range of architectural styles that could be purchased by prospective homeowners and residential builders.

Using the plan book as a vehicle for her work, Wilburn not only responded to the acute housing shortage in urban areas but also addressed the need for affordable, well-designed houses in rural communities. In her third plan book, *Ideal Homes of Today*, Wilburn expressed her abiding desire to provide homes for southerners throughout the region, stating: "The idea of publishing house designs, so that the builder in the small town may have a home in as good taste as his city brother, has always appealed to me."[1] For decades her mail-order house designs were popular among realtors, builders, and homeowners in both cities and small towns, where Wilburn's plan book houses influenced residential development and supported homeownership for the middle class.

This chapter examines the plan designs published in Wilburn's first five plan books and some representative houses built from them. It shows how Wilburn created not only a successful plan book business but also a substantial and lasting architectural legacy.[2] As we consider architectural designs of individual plan book houses in detail, we will see that supplying affordable house designs for the middle class was not Wilburn's most important professional accomplishment. Rather, Wilburn's greatest achievements are reflected in the aesthetic and

FIGURE 2.1. This view of Adams Street in the MAK Historic District in Decatur, Ga., offers a glimpse of an historic neighborhood developed as one of the first subdivisions in Decatur in the early twentieth century. The neighborhood includes many southern homes that were designed by Wilburn and offered as mail-order house plans in Wilburn's first plan book, *Southern Homes and Bungalows* (1914).

practical quality of her plan book designs and experienced in the hundreds of well-designed homes built from her mail-order plans. Her enduring architectural legacy includes the contributions she made in designing homes to be efficient and comfortable, practical and spacious, simple, economical, and also beautiful. Offered as plan book houses, they reflected her keen understanding and deep appreciation of people, place, and culture.

Designed as smaller, more modern homes for the middle class in the twentieth century, Wilburn's plan book houses have become attractive, historic homes in the twenty-first century. Many are located in local historic districts as well as National Register Historic Districts throughout the Atlanta area.[3] As can be seen in the example shown in Figure 2.1, they contribute to the historic character and charm of many southern neighborhoods. They were built from mail-order house plans that reflected a southerner's understanding of comfort, a designer's response to climate, and a woman's understanding of household needs. For generations, these homes have adapted to new technologies and changing times, and they have been appreciated and enjoyed for generations as homes that offer southern comfort, American style.

In the introduction to her first plan book, Wilburn affirmed her ambition to design homes for southerners, the people she knew best, and to supply house plans that were responsive to the climate of the Southeast. She wrote, "This book is published with the idea of supplying Southern people with homes suitable for climatic conditions of the Southeast."[4] As a native southerner, Wilburn understood the importance of designing homes that were responsive to the South's hot, humid summers and mild winter months. As a plan book architect, she provided houses that were designed for climate, with features that promoted comfort and offered convenience throughout the year.

In the first decades of the twentieth century, most homes in the South were built with fireplaces as the primary source of heating. Wood or coal-burning fireplaces heated most living spaces, including bedrooms. Typically, each room was designed so that it could be heated individually and closed off when not in use (or to conserve heat). In Wilburn's first plan book, houses included fireplace heating and also were designed to accommodate the "modern convenience" of a central heating system, as furnace and boiler systems were becoming more affordable and thus more common in middle-class residences. Basements or lower-level service areas typically provided spaces for these central heating systems, which could supply heat to all rooms, allowing interior living spaces to be more open. Living rooms, parlors, dining areas, sun rooms, and other adjacent first-level spaces often were connected with wide doorways. Pocket doors or French doors allowed these spaces to be opened up or combined to function as a larger living area for social events, providing greater flexibility.

Long, hot, humid summers posed greater design challenges than the South's mild winters during these decades before central air conditioning.[5] In designing for southern comfort in warmer months, Wilburn made use of central halls, high ceilings, large, operable windows, and wide interior doorways to provide good ventilation so that interior spaces would remain cooler than outside temperatures. In many house designs, Wilburn located bedrooms in corner spaces in order to have windows on two sides of the room, promoting cross-ventilation, good air movement,

and balanced natural light. Sleeping porches, which were popular features in early twentieth-century houses, were offered in many of Wilburn's early plan book houses. The flexibility in function offered by wide doorways between living spaces on the first level also allowed rooms to be opened up in summer months, providing greater cross-ventilation and air circulation for cooling interior spaces.

By the late nineteenth century, large Victorian homes with highly decorative exteriors and elaborate interiors were beginning to be replaced with more popular European historical styles, which offered simpler forms and more refined exteriors. Instead of the highly ornamental Victorian homes, European-inspired houses that drew on historical precedents for style and inspiration became more popular in what is known as the first phase of the eclectic period in American architectural history. As historian Virginia McAlester explained in *A Field Guide to American Houses*, the eclectic period lasted approximately from 1880 to 1940 and "draws on the full spectrum of Western architectural tradition—Ancient Classical, Medieval, and Renaissance Classical—for stylistic inspiration. Unlike the free stylistic mixtures that had dominated the preceding Victorian era, the Eclectic movement stresses relatively pure copies of domestic architecture as originally built in various European countries and their New World colonies."[6] In the early part of this period, architects designed custom homes with the popular architectural features of historical European styles, rather than the decorative features of their predecessors. In the early 1900s, however, the movement evolved, as the demand for designs for more economical houses equipped with modern household technologies led to the sudden rise in the popularity of smaller, more practical houses. These modern houses, represented by the prairie and craftsman styles, emphasized functionality, efficiency, and economy more than decorative features and particular characteristics of historical styles.[7] As McAlester explained, "In the first two decades of the 20th century this first phase was interrupted and almost overwhelmed by the first wave of architectural modernism presented by Craftsman and Prairie styles with their purely American origins."[8]

As early twentieth-century, American house styles, the craftsman and the prairie styles were characterized by compact floor plans, informal living spaces, new building technologies, and household improvements. The reordering of priorities in residential design that contributed to their popularity was influenced to some extent by the added costs for these new household technologies and improvements, such as lighting, heating, and plumbing systems. Because these improvements increased construction costs, the demand for economical house designs that were smaller in size, simpler in plan and style, and thus more affordable for homeowners increased accordingly.[9]

Southern Homes and Bungalows, Wilburn's first plan book, included mail-order houses designs in two dominant house types—the "southern home" and the "bungalow." Wilburn offered versions of these types predominantly in the popular eclectic, colonial revival, and craftsman styles. The post-Victorian southern home and the smaller one-story bungalow represented modern homes for new, twentieth-century suburbs. With large porches, an abundance of windows, and strong connections to the outdoors, the southern home and bungalow also were house types particularly well-suited to the mild climate of the Southeast.[10]

In her early plan books, Wilburn used the term "southern home" to describe her plan designs for the post-Victorian, two-story houses that reflected popular architectural styles. Wilburn's "southern home" as a house type was based on the American vernacular four-square house form, with typically four rooms on each level and a simple rectilinear floor plan. Designed as a mail-order stock plan and offered as an economical design, the southern home was not a true replication of a historical style. Instead, the southern home had a plain exterior, typically wood siding with a brick or stone foundation, columns, and large chimneys. Rather than expensive, custom-designed details, this house type featured a combination of natural materials and stock building components in simpler eclectic, colonial revival, or craftsman style designs, much like other stock house plans offered through companies and popular publications of the period.

The house shown in Figure 2.2 has many of the typical features of Wilburn's plan book designs for southern homes. Based on the four-square house type, this house has a large stone foundation with wood siding and a nine-room floor plan with spacious living areas connected by wide openings and pocket doors, as can be seen in the floor plan, shown in Figure 2.3. Each main room had fireplace heating. The boxed eaves, projecting cross gable, large windows, porch columns, and railings are among the beautifully crafted exterior details that suggest a colonial revival influence on this post-Victorian southern home.

In her first three plan books, Wilburn offered a number of bungalow designs that were popular as smaller houses, offering simplicity, economy, and convenience. As a house type, the bungalow was a one-story structure characterized by a low roof line, wide roof overhangs with roof brackets, a large front porch or veranda, and grouped windows, with wood, brick, and stone exteriors. This vernacular house type was often built in the craftsman style, which had been popularized by the arts and crafts movement.[11] However, the bungalow house type often was designed with architectural features characteristic of other styles, such as the colonial revival style.

In describing the southern homes and bungalows offered in her first plan book, Wilburn wrote in the volume's introduction:

> The designs shown in most books of this kind show houses with small rooms and no fireplaces, low roofs and too fancy construction. Here will be found plans for moderate-cost residences where the influence of the English half-timber cottage, the Swiss Chalet and the Mission Bungalow is felt. Usually a combination of the above styles results in a conglomerate which is incongruous and inartistic, but in selecting the homes for this publication only those of good plan arrangement and sensible construction have been used.[12]

FIGURE 2.2. This historic home on Adams Street in Decatur, Ga., was built from plan design no. 628 in *Southern Homes and Bungalows*. It is an outstanding example of an early two-story southern home and was one of Wilburn's earliest plan book houses.

As Wilburn explained, her early plan book house designs used architectural features and materials reminiscent of European-inspired historical styles and the craftsman style, following popular trends. Such styles responded to the increased demand for plainer, more economical houses for the middle class. They represented a more popular form of eclecticism, which emerged in the early 1900s through the 1920s, that McAlester describes as "the first wave of architectural modernism."[13] These early modern American houses were designed for greater functionality, efficiency, comfort, and simplicity (more than to conform to or replicate a particular

Design No. 628

THE exterior lines of this house are all that could be asked for. Although the house is square in shape the slight projections on each side relieve the monotony. The massive rubble stone foundation together with the unusually large columns and broad eaves give a most substantial effect.

The room arrangement is good, the three main rooms being connected by sliding doors so that these rooms can be made into practically one large room. As the stair is in the rear hall and a portiere can be used at the cased opening, no rear stair is needed.

FIGURE 2.3. Plan design no. 628 was one of the few in Wilburn's first plan book to offer a downstairs bedroom in addition to four bedrooms and a bath on the second level. The large veranda and open terrace provided large, outdoor living spaces along the front of the house.

historical style), responding to the demand for smaller, more compact house plans for newly developed suburbs and neighborhoods. According to McAlester, the craftsman style "was the dominant style for smaller houses built throughout the country during the period from about 1905 until the early 1920s."[14]

After serving in the Army civilian service from 1917 to 1918 during World War I, Wilburn resumed her architectural practice in Atlanta and continued to provide house plans that addressed the need for smaller, more economical, and more modern homes for the middle class. Soon after her return, she published her second plan book, *Brick and Colonial Homes* (1921), offering it as "a collection of the latest designs, featuring the most modern in domestic architecture."[15] In supplying a variety of house plans in a range of sizes, materials, and architectural styles, Wilburn addressed an unprecedented need for well-designed southern homes. The foreword, shown in Figure 2.4, represents the first time that she provides in a plan book a full description of her work, building advice to homeowners, and an explanation of her business practices as a plan book architect.

Support for the new trends in residential design and desire for housing reform was widespread in the first decades of the twentieth century. Many popular magazines and publications advocated for smaller, more economical house designs that increased efficiencies and reduced household labor and expenses.[16]

The architectural designs in Wilburn's early plan books exemplified the new priorities and popular trends in the design of the modern home. As popular house designs, they reflected progressive ideals and incorporated

FIGURE 2.4. The foreword to Wilburn's second plan book, *Brick and Colonial Homes*, offers her first detailed explanation of her business practices and some advice to builders and homeowners. Similar information was also published in later plan books.

FOREWORD

IN PRESENTING the group of homes shown on the following pages, the idea has been to submit a variety of designs and floor plans which may at least assist you, as a prospective builder, in arriving at about what you want.

What we most need in America is a better class of small domestic architecture, one which shall provide us with homes more wholesome in their external appearance and more satisfying in their internal arrangement and finish.

The building of a home is an important event in any life. That's the very best reason you can find for planning carefully every feature of your house. Some say, "Never mind the exterior, I live inside—not outside. Give me a beautiful interior and my neighbors will have to put up with the outside." This is not right. We owe something to our neighbors; we do care what they think of the appearance of our home, and the ideal home is a well-balanced structure, harmonious in detail, and attractive outside as well as inside. Those houses which have that "indescribable something" are, after all, an expression of the owner's individuality.

MATERIALS AND DESIGNS

In making for comfort and security, the enclosing walls are all-important. So, in planning your home do not put all the stress on the floor arrangement. No matter if you are building with no intention of selling, do not make the house freakish, as salability should always be considered. You aren't going to build very often in your lifetime so consider the materials to be used.

BRICK:

There is nothing which will give the house so much dignity, stability and permanency as brick. To some of us brick means the old style common brick, while to others of us it stands for a building material that only the richest can afford. The extra cost for veneering a house with face brick is very little when one takes into consideration that with brick outside walls the insurance rate is lower; the house is cooler in summer and warmer in winter; and the cost of upkeep is materially reduced. Now that the newer tapestry brick can be had in such rich and varied finishes and colorings, some most pleasing exteriors are now obtainable in brick homes.

FRAME:

The frame house needs no introduction, it is suitable for many localities, can be made most attractive, and on account of the low cost is one of the most popular materials of which to build. It is only in comparatively recent years that the more discerning public has turned with appreciation and respect to the beauty of the early Colonial traditions. In the new Colonial homes boxed eaves are used as well as the ones with exposed rafter ends, the stoop at the entrance gives access to the house so that the side porch, now so often seen, may be private. Homes of this design, although not always purely Colonial, show a touch of that type here and there, which, added to the general simplicity of the design, makes a home that is not only distinctive, but one that will withstand the critical test of time.

STUCCO:

The last few years have seen an increasing use of stucco over both frame and hollow tile. A well built stucco house is attractive, is lasting, comfortable and its cost is not prohibitive. The "up-keep" is less than with the weather-boarded house and although it need never be painted its color can be changed by the use of specially prepared paints. In brick houses stucco is much in demand for use in the gable ends. Colonial, Spanish and Italian designs can be well carried out where stucco is used for exterior finish.

INTERIORS:

The Colonial, brick and stucco homes, in so far as arrangement of rooms is concerned, are no different from any other type. In the more recent homes French doors between rooms take the place of sliding doors or colonades; a simple cornice moulding is used instead of the old beamed ceilings; and the dining rooms have the walls paneled by nailing a small mould directly to the plastered wall, this being used instead of the old "dust catching" plate rail. See other building ideas at the bottom of each page.

WHAT PLANS INCLUDE

For the past fifteen years I have spent my vacations visiting other cities, have taken over 5,000 kodak pictures, made sketches and bought books so as to keep myself well posted on every new feature in home architecture. I feel that, being a woman, I know just the little things that should go in a house to make living in it a pleasure to the entire family.

The plans shown in this book are my personal designs; they are not photographs of other architect's work. Many of the houses have been built several times and builders will find that they "work out" correctly. All room sizes show inside measurements.

PLANS:

The plans are practical working drawings, made to a scale of 1/4" to the foot and furnished you in blueprint form. They cover foundation, floor and roof plan, exterior elevations and details (to a larger scale) of exterior mill work and interior built-in features. The specifications are specially prepared for each house, supplement the drawings, and cover the masonry, plastering, carpentry, hardware, electric work, screens, plumbing, heating, metal work, painting, etc.

LUMBER AND MILL LISTS:

The lumber list is particularly useful where you wish to saw your framing before you begin to buy other material. The lists also assure you that all supply men are bidding on the same quality and amounts. The lists give the size, length and number of pieces of all framing and the size and quantity of all mill work such as doors, windows, flooring, shingles, laths, and built-in-features.

REVERSE PLANS:

This means that all rooms shown on left will be on the right and all on the right will be on the left; everything is reversed, plans are redrawn so that lettering reads correctly. Note this when looking over the designs as sometimes the reversed plan will "be just what you want" when the plan as shown would not do at all.

SPECIAL PLANS

In case you want a design somewhat different from any shown herein, pick out the one most like what you want, send me the plan number and a sketch or description of the way you want it changed; it may be that among my other plans I will find one that will appeal to you, thus saving the cost of a new design.

If not, I will quote you prices for plans made to your order if so instructed. For special plans pencil sketches are always sent for your criticism and correction, the final plans are not completed until drawings are made which meet your approval. With new plans you get three complete sets of blueprinted plans and typewriten specifications. A separate price is given for the lumber and mill list as this may be ordered or not as desired. In ordering new plans give size of lot, whether inside or on a corner, way it faces and whether level or sloping.

CONSTRUCTION COSTS

The cost question for years will be more or less problematical. For this reason I am not giving any estimated costs. Select the plan you desire to build, order plans and have your contractor give you a bid for the completed job.

PAYMENT

Money order or personal check should accompany all orders for ready drawn plans. If preferable plans will be sent by express, C. O. D., with privilege of examination.

OTHER PLAN BOOKS

I have published two other plan books that I will be glad to furnish you: Southern Homes and Bungalows, 8x11 size, 80 designs, price 75c. Up-to-date Homes, 5x7 size, 24 designs, price 25c. Folder, "Successful Homes," 17 designs, free.

Be sure you get a perfect title to your lot

modern technologies, offering comfort, simplicity, economy, and efficiency in a variety of architectural styles and plan arrangements.

Stylistically, most of the two-story southern homes in Wilburn's early plan book designs were characterized by simple, rectilinear floor plans, based on the American four-square house type. With less ornamentation and scrollwork than the more ornate, decorative styles of the Victorian era, Wilburn's southern homes ranged from plain wood-frame structures with large verandas across the front and second-level sleeping porches to European-inspired eclectic style houses with brick façades, prominent side porches, and light-filled interiors. All were simple in form and plan arrangement, with beautifully crafted details, spacious interiors, and flexible living spaces. Similarly, Wilburn's bungalow designs were one- or one-and-a-half-story plans, typically clad in wood-frame, masonry, or a combination of these materials for structure and exterior façades, much like other typical bungalow designs of the period.

The large porch, a prominent architectural feature of both the southern home and the bungalow, was perhaps Wilburn's most prevalent design response to climate and culture. In Wilburn's plan book designs, the front porch was an outdoor living room that functioned as a comfortable sitting area and a social gathering space. It also served as an important transition space from the street to the residence, offering a covered place for arrivals and departures. In Wilburn's early two-story house designs, the front porch often extended the entire length of the house, and it was one of the most attractive and prominent features of these southern homes. In period houses of the 1920s and 1930s, particularly the colonial revival style, the porch space often was located on the side of the house, often serving as a screen porch or sunroom, with a direct connection to an indoor living area.

Before the development of residential air conditioning systems, the front porch functioned in the South as an essential living space, providing a comfortable sitting area that was shaded from the sun and open to breezes. Often called a veranda in Wilburn's plan books, the front porch was designed for the southern climate but also developed in response to certain aspects of southern culture and social life. Traditionally, it functioned as a favorite gathering place, particularly in late summer afternoons and evenings, when cooler outdoor temperatures and breezes often made the porch a more pleasant space than a home's interior. Typically furnished with seating, often a porch swing at one end, as well as tables and chairs, the front porch was a place of recreation, relaxation, conversations, and social events. Wilburn often referred to the porch as "a summer living room."[17] Figure 2.5 shows an example of a typical front porch on one of Wilburn's southern homes, furnished with seating, tables, and a porch swing.

FIGURE 2.5. The front porch on Wilburn's southern homes was typically designed as the main entrance to the home and as an attractive, outdoor living room, with a generous seating area to accommodate furnishings.

Large porches or verandas that extended across the front of the house, with front steps located on the far left or right side, allowed residents and guests to access the front door without walking through the living space. This design strategy was common in many of Wilburn's designs, including plan design no. 715 shown in Figure 2.6. Front porch steps led to an entrance at one end of the porch. As Wilburn explained, "The porch is large and arranged so that people on the veranda are not disturbed by those passing from the front steps to door."[18] For plan design no. 842, a

southern home shown in Figure 2.7, Wilburn called attention to the convenience afforded by this strategy, stating: "The veranda, with its entrance at one end, leaves the main part so that it can be fitted up as a summer living room."[19]

Built on Adams Street in Decatur, Georgia, and published in Wilburn's first plan book, plan design no. 656 is another example of a two-story southern home with a veranda designed as an outdoor living room, as shown in Figure 2.8. The veranda is thirty-one feet long. Its twelve-foot

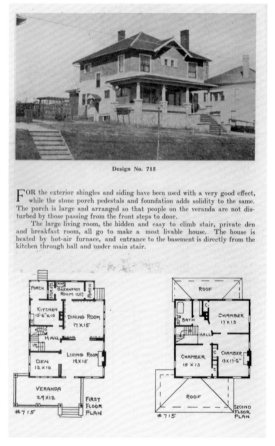

FIGURE 2.6. Plan design no. 715 in *Southern Homes and Bungalows* featured an eight-room southern home with a small den connected to the living room across the front of the house. It was one of the first house plans to offer a central heating system, with a furnace located in the basement.

FIGURE 2.7. Plan design no. 842 in *Southern Homes and Bungalows* was a typical two-story southern home, with a prominent veranda and an eight-room floor plan that included three bedrooms and a sleeping porch on the second level.

Design No. 656

TAKEN in all this home is most attractive, and shows a design with a distinct individuality without being at all "freakish." The grouping of the square and round columns give a decided departure from the usual sameness of veranda work.

The interior is ideal, both in attractiveness and in its supply of the conveniences that go to make this such a desirable home. The library may be shut off completely from the living room and used as a bed room. The coat room, with the lavatory in it, will be found to save many steps, as will the central pass pantry, allowing access from the kitchen to the front door without passing through the dining room.

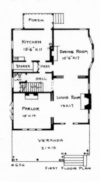

FIGURE 2.8. This two-story southern home was built on Adams Street in Decatur, Ga., from plan design no. 656. Like most of Wilburn's southern homes, it had a simple form and plan arrangement, based on the vernacular, four-square house type.

depth easily accommodated furnishings for an outdoor living area. A two-story house with spacious interiors, plan design no. 656 offered an eight-room floor plan similar to many other plan designs for two-story southern homes, as shown in Figure 2.9. It featured four main rooms on each level, with living spaces on the first level that usually included a living room, a dining room, a parlor/library, and a kitchen. The second level was designed with three or four very large chambers (bedrooms), a sleeping porch, and a hallway bath.

FIGURE 2.9. Plan design no. 656 in *Southern Homes and Bungalows* was distinguished by double columns on the large veranda that extended across the front of the house. The two-story, eight-room plan included a spacious interior. On the first level the parlor, living, and dining rooms were connected by wide openings and pocket doors.

FIGURE 2.10. This two-story southern home was built on Adams Street in Decatur from plan design no. 715. Its stone foundation, prominent front steps, and porch railing are distinguishing architectural features that give the house dignity and charm.

Wilburn used the four-square house form and eight-room plan in designing many plan book houses in a variety of different architectural styles. The simple rectilinear or square form offered spacious interiors with living areas on the first-level and corner bedrooms and private spaces on the second level. Large windows provided an abundance of fresh air and daylight in all rooms, and back porches and basements accommodated practical service and storage needs. Figure 2.10 shows a house on Adams Street in Decatur, Georgia, that was built from a four-square, southern home plan design (no. 715) in Wilburn's first plan book (see Fig. 2.6 for the plan).

The plan book design shown in Figure 2.11, plan design no. 609, is another typical two-story southern home offered in Wilburn's first plan book. On the first level, large openings and pocket doors between the front parlor, living room, and dining room allowed residents to use rooms separately for specific functions or to open up the rooms for entertaining or hosting large gatherings. The second level included three large bedrooms, a smaller bedroom, balcony, and hall bath. It also had a large veranda designed so that it could be furnished and used as an outdoor living room. Its distinguishing exterior features included heavy porch columns and a pergola that wrapped around the front of the house over an outdoor terrace at grade. Wilburn described it as follows:

> The above house is laid out on dignified lines and is one well adapted to any locality. The tapestry brick foundation, trellis work, heavy columns, and pergola effect to veranda roof gives the house an individual appearance. Nothing has been omitted that is necessary to good living. The side entrance will be found a great convenience. The rooms are all of ample size and the three main first floor rooms can be thrown well together. As the stair is partly hidden no rear stairway is necessary. The second floor has four bed rooms with closets to each, a linen closet and a large storage room. The balcony is arranged for out-of-door sleeping in summer. A servants' room besides the furnace and coal rooms are to be found in the basement.[20]

Built-in furnishings, including window seats in the living room, and a built-in china cabinet in the breakfast room were among the popular features offered in plan design no. 609, as shown in Figure 2.11. A large pantry adjacent to the kitchen also offered convenient storage on the first level. The second level was designed with three large corner chambers (bedrooms), a hallway bath, a smaller chamber, and a rear balcony. All living spaces and upstairs bedrooms had fireplace heating in addition to a coal-burning furnace in the basement. Figure 2.12 shows a house built on Adams Street in Decatur, Georgia, from this plan.

As shown in these examples, Wilburn's early plan book designs offered comfortable, spacious rooms for entertaining, functional service areas to support daily activities, and large bedrooms that provided privacy

Design No. 609

THE above house is laid out on dignified lines and is one well adapted to any locality. The tapestry brick foundation, trellis work, heavy columns, and pergola effect to veranda roof give the house an individual appearance. Nothing has been omitted that is necessary to good living. The side entrance will be found a great convenience. The rooms are all of ample size and the three main first floor rooms can be thrown well together. As the stair is partly hidden no rear stairway is necessary. The second floor has four bed rooms with closets to each, a linen closet and a large storage room. The balcony is arranged for out-of-door sleeping in summer. A servants' room besides the furnace and coal rooms are to be found in the basement.

FIGURE 2.11. Plan design no. 609 in *Southern Homes and Bungalows* was a larger southern home. This plan design featured built-in furnishings in the living room, breakfast room, and kitchen, and it had a basement to house the furnace and coal room for the central heating system.

FIGURE 2.12. This southern home was built on Adams Street in Decatur, Ga., from plan design no. 609. The large porch columns and porch railing were among the attractive design features of this large, two-story residence.

and separation from the main living areas. All rooms were designed to take advantage of day lighting, cross-ventilation, and views. In describing her plan book houses, Wilburn claimed special expertise as a woman in designing houses that offered convenience, efficiency, comfort, and style, stating: "I feel that, being a woman, I know just the little things that should go in a house to make living in it a pleasure to the entire family."[21] Although her claim was likely a marketing strategy, her floor plans and architectural designs clearly demonstrated her expertise in designing practical, functional spaces for diverse households. They also reflected her understanding and appreciation of space needs and everyday functions, particularly the needs for adequate service, support, and storage spaces. Basements were typical service areas included in many of Wilburn's stock plans, and Wilburn designed them to provide space for laundry areas, heating equipment, and servant's rooms. Designs for large trunk rooms, linen closets, laundry spaces, pantries, sewing rooms, and other service and support spaces further demonstrated Wilburn's expertise in providing spaces that offered efficiency, convenience, and flexibility.

Wilburn also recognized the importance of designing rooms so that they could serve multiple purposes and thus be used as flexible living spaces. This design strategy was popular among builders and architects, as well as among advocates of the ideal progressive house and modern house designs. Instead of having living spaces with separate functions, Wilburn designed such spaces to serve multiple functions, thus increasing their functionality and the overall efficiency of the home. For example, built-in fold-down beds allowed living spaces to be also used for sleeping. Libraries and dens were other living spaces designed to serve multiple functions or that could be adapted easily to serve a different function. Wilburn often designed a dining room or parlor so that it also could function as a downstairs bedroom, or a sewing room on the second level that could be converted into a children's bedroom.

In describing the change from single to multi-purpose functions for the living room in the early-twentieth-century modern home, historian Gwendolyn Wright explained: "A room that was seldom used meant a waste of precious household space. The multiple-purpose living room absorbed the variety of settings for entertaining of the Victorian dwelling—the parlor, living hall, sitting room, family room—into a single space."[22] The living room in plan design no. 303, shown in Figure 2.37, like many in Wilburn's two-story southern homes, was designed to serve multiple functions as the primary living space. This plan design also was designed so that the sun room with an adjacent bath could function as a downstairs bedroom, providing flexibility in accommodating changing household needs.

Plan design no. 587, shown in Figure 2.13, is an outstanding example of a smaller southern home that offered a compact floor plan with many architectural features that provide charm and character. Wilburn described this three-bedroom home as follows:

> In this two-story house one gets a great deal for a little money. The walls of stained siding below and shingles above, together with the bracketed cornice, give an individual appearance to the exterior. The broad veranda gives ample porch room and the heavy columns are quite effective. The stairway in the living room was particularly designed to add to the spacious air of the first floor. The rooms are heated by fire-place, but if a basement were desired for furnace heat an entrance from the inside of the house to the basement could be made under the main stairway. On the second floor three bed rooms, bath, trunk room, and sleeping porch are well grouped.[23]

The exterior had large wooden columns on masonry pedestals with a veranda extending the entire length of the house. A large staircase with a window seat in the living room was a prominent feature with large pocket doors connecting the living area to the dining room across the front of the house. Figure 2.14 shows a house built from this plan design that is on Jefferson Place in Decatur.

Design No. 587

IN THIS two-story house one gets a great deal for a little money. The walls of stained siding below and shingles above, together with the bracketed cornice, give an individual appearance to the exterior. The broad veranda gives ample porch room and the heavy columns are quite effective. The stairway in the living room was particularly designed to add to the spacious air of the first floor. The rooms are heated by fire-place, but if a basement were desired for furnace heat an entrance from the inside of the house to the basement could be made under the main stairway. On the second floor three bed rooms, bath, trunk room and sleeping porch are well grouped.

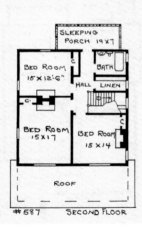

FIGURE 2.13. As one of the smaller, two-story southern homes, plan design no. 587 in *Southern Homes and Bungalows* offered a spacious interior with a compact floor plan. A beautiful open staircase with a built-in seat was a prominent feature in the living room.

FIGURE 2.14. This craftsman style southern home was built on Jefferson Place in Decatur, Ga., from plan design no. 587. Craftsman features included a stone foundation, exposed roof brackets, and tapered porch columns. The exterior had wood siding on the first level and wood shingles on the second level.

Southern Homes and Bungalows was the only plan book that included photographs of interior architectural features such as a colonnade, a stair, a fireplace, and a winding stairway with a built-in seat. Many plan designs in this plan book also included built-in furnishings that provided economical, practical storage spaces that were popular features in the early modern home. Bookcases, china cabinets, and built-in seating areas were designed to fit discreetly into the overall room plan and were intended to replace the large buffets, armoires, and other heavy furnishings of the Victorian era. Living spaces often had built-in bookshelves and window seats; dining rooms and breakfast rooms featured built-in cabinets for china storage. In her first plan book, Wilburn wrote: "All cozy corners and jig-saw work have been abolished and in place is found such useful built-in furniture and artistic effects as book-cases, window seats, buffets, plate rails, concealed beds, ironing boards, colonnades and beamed ceilings."[24] Built-in furnishings also were economical and practical, expressing the modern aesthetic that celebrated simplicity and practicality. In her description of a six-room bungalow house design (plan design no. 780) in *Southern Homes and Bungalows*, Wilburn emphasized the savings that these furnishings would allow: "The rooms are all of good size and will furnish without much expense as there are many pieces of built-in furniture."[25]

Except for closets and cupboards, many built-in features became less popular after 1920, as construction costs increased and the cost of home furnishings decreased.[26] Wilburn's later plans, which had fewer built-in features, reflected this evolution in interior features and furnishings.

Fold-out beds, which allowed a homeowner to convert a living space into a bedroom, promoted flexibility and efficiency and were featured in several of Wilburn's early house plans. Figure 2.15 includes an advertisement for Murphy In-a-Dor beds from Wilburn's first plan book printed on the same page as plan design no. 1177, which featured fold-down beds shown in the floor plan.

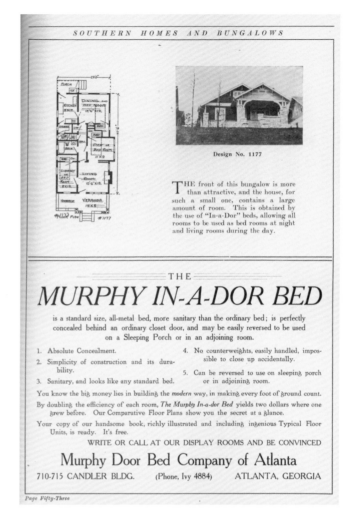

FIGURE 2.15. This advertisement for a Murphy In-a-Dor Bed—a built-in furnishing that could be used to convert living spaces to bedrooms— appeared in Wilburn's first plan book, *Southern Homes and Bungalows*. Plan design no. 1177, at the top of the page, had fold-down beds shown in the floor plan as an example of how they could allow "all rooms to be used as bed rooms at night and living rooms during the day."

Design No. 876

THIS stucco house is one of the most pleasing in design shown. The house is square in shape and therefore not expensive to build. The interior arrangements are all that could be desired. The central hall connects with the dining room, living room and library, the last two opening out upon the sun parlor. The first floor lavatory and two baths give most desirable plumbing arrangements. The rear and attic stairs are well located.

FIGURE 2.16. Plan design no. 876 in *Southern Homes and Bungalows* was designed as a stucco house with a formal entrance hall on the first level. The house featured a large library behind the living room with built-in seating and a sun parlor with French doors to the library and living-room spaces.

FIGURE 2.17. Built from plan design no. 876 on Springdale Road in the Druid Hills neighborhood in Atlanta, this home is an outstanding example of one of Wilburn's early plan book houses. It is the only home known to have been built in this neighborhood from a plan design in Wilburn's first plan book.

As mentioned previously, many of Wilburn's southern homes used the economical four-square plan and form, which provided an efficient plan arrangement and a simple rectilinear form. An early example, featuring one of Wilburn's larger southern homes, is plan design no. 876, a stucco house that was offered in *Southern Homes and Bungalows* (see Fig. 2.16). Wilburn described the house design as "square in shape and therefore not expensive to build."[27] Figure 2.17 shows a southern home built from this plan that features a veranda extending across the entire front of the house with a symmetrically placed front door opening into a formal entrance hall and stair hall. Kitchen and dining spaces were located on one side of the hall. A large living room on the front of the house connected to a large library (16 x 15 feet) with a built-in window seat and bookcases behind the living room. An open outdoor terrace connected the veranda to a side sun parlor, which had direct connections to the library and living room. The second floor had three large corner bedrooms with two baths, closet spaces, and a sleeping porch. A separate service stair connected the rear hall and kitchen with the second level. A half bath was located off the rear hall near the back porch. The bedrooms were large enough to be furnished with a sitting area in addition to the bed and furniture for clothes storage. Although the third level is not shown in the plan, the service stair extended to the attic, which had a full height dormer and likely was used for storage space. The two-story, symmetrical stucco façade, stone foundation, large porch, high ceilings, central hall, and spacious floor plan were among the attractive features in this house design, which was grander in size and scale than many of the southern homes in Wilburn's first plan book.

As shown in Figure 2.18, plan design no. 674 was a more typical two-story southern home design featured in Wilburn's first plan book. This house, while smaller in scale and size than the house in Figure 2.17, also had a symmetrical façade and a large front porch extending across the front of the house. Rooms were smaller in this design with a more compact floor plan that had no entry hall or stair hall. Wilburn wrote of this plan: "The turned porch columns resting on pedestals of tapestry brick and the central gable, together with the wide overhanging eaves, add a quiet dignity to the front of this house. There are ten rooms, the three main rooms on the first floor being arranged so as to be thrown together into one large room by means of the connecting sliding doors. The sleeping porch and many large closets make the second floor most complete."[28] The floor plan is typical of many of Wilburn's southern homes, with living spaces connected by sliding, pocket doors on the first level and large bedrooms, closets, and a sleeping porch on the second level.

Although Wilburn's first plan book offered many two-story southern homes as post-Victorian houses, most of the mail-order house designs in

THE turned porch columns resting on pedestals of tapestry brick and the central gable, together with the wide overhanging eaves, add a quiet dignity to the front of this house. There are ten rooms, the three main rooms on the first floor being arranged so as to be thrown into one large room by means of the connecting sliding doors. The sleeping porch and many large closets make the second floor most complete.

Design No. 674

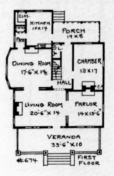
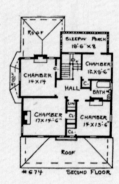

FIGURE 2.18. Plan design no. 674 in *Southern Homes and Bungalows* was designed as a post-Victorian southern home with a symmetrical façade and a large veranda across the front. Its attractive features included the turned porch columns and railing and a large bay window in the dining room.

Southern Homes and Bungalows were bungalow plans. Bungalow plan designs were also offered in Wilburn's second and third plan books. Designed initially for the mild California climate, the bungalow was one of many early modern house types that emphasized comfort, efficiency, and functionality more than historical styles at the turn of the century.[29] With its simple rectilinear form and efficient plan arrangement, it was affordable as well as attractive, and it quickly became popular with homeowners throughout the country. Figures 2.19, 2.20, 2.22, and 2.24 show examples of craftsman bungalow designs from Wilburn's early plan books.

The typical bungalow floor plan had a living, dining, kitchen, and back porch space on one side of the house, and the private areas—two or three bedrooms and one bath—on the other side. The floor plan was open, with living areas connected by French doors, pocket doors, or wide openings, which made it functional and flexible for household gatherings and activities. Built-in furnishings in living and dining areas, as well as features such as fold-down beds, reduced the need for furniture and increased the functionality and flexibility of these smaller houses. Figure 2.19 provides an example of a craftsman bungalow design with many of these characteristics. Wilburn described it as follows:

> Taken in all, this is a most attractive bungalow, having a distinct individuality without being at all freakish. The large front porch has been made to extend the entire width of house so as to give ample space for use as a summer living room. For the exterior, painted siding and light green stained shingles have been used with a very good effect, while the stone porch columns add solidity to the same. Unlike the majority of bungalows, this one is painted white, and a more cheerful, wholesome color could not be had. This is an ideal bungalow for a family requiring three bed rooms. The front bed room is so arranged that it may be completely cut off from the living room.[30]

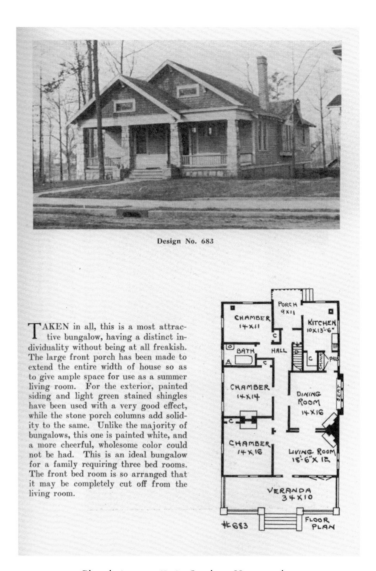

Design No. 683

TAKEN in all, this is a most attractive bungalow, having a distinct individuality without being at all freakish. The large front porch has been made to extend the entire width of house so as to give ample space for use as a summer living room. For the exterior, painted siding and light green stained shingles have been used with a very good effect, while the stone porch columns add solidity to the same. Unlike the majority of bungalows, this one is painted white, and a more cheerful, wholesome color could not be had. This is an ideal bungalow for a family requiring three bed rooms. The front bed room is so arranged that it may be completely cut off from the living room.

FIGURE 2.19. Plan design no. 683 in *Southern Homes and Bungalows* was designed as a one-story, three-bedroom craftsman bungalow. Built-in furnishings included a window seat in the dining room and a built-in china cabinet.

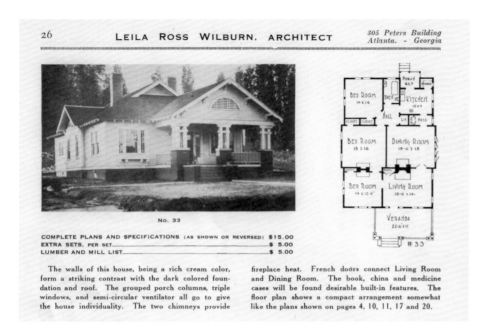

FIGURE 2.20. Plan design no. 33 in *Brick and Colonial Homes* was a craftsman bungalow design with heavy, double porch columns. The columns' unusual capitals gave the house a distinct appearance. The compact floor plan included fireplace heating and built-in furnishings, and was a typical design for a six-room bungalow.

FIGURE 2.21. This craftsman bungalow on King's Highway in Decatur, Ga., was built from plan design no. 33. Its front porch columns represent one of the most original architectural features on this craftsman bungalow.

Plan design no. 33, a craftsman bungalow in Wilburn's second plan book, *Brick and Colonial Homes*, had a masonry foundation, wood clapboard siding, and a prominent cross gable porch extending across the front of the house. As shown in Figure 2.20, the double porch columns rested on masonry pedestal foundations and had prominent double column capitals with horizontal crosspieces. Wilburn called attention to this unique feature, stating: "The walls of this house, being a rich cream color, form a striking contrast with the dark colored foundation and roof. The grouped porch columns, triple windows, and semi-circular ventilator all go to give the house individuality. The two chimneys provide fireplace heat. French

doors connect Living Room and Dining Room. The book, china and medicine cases will be found desirable built-in features."[31] This house design was built on King's Highway, in the McDonough–Adams St.–King's Highway (MAK) Historic District in Decatur, Georgia, as shown in Figure 2.21.

A popular bungalow design offered in *Brick and Colonial Homes*, plan design no. 8 was built in many neighborhoods in the Atlanta area, including Candler Park, Decatur, and Midtown. Wilburn described this plan as being one of her most popular designs. It was offered as a six-room bungalow with two bedrooms and a sleeping porch. Figure 2.22 shows

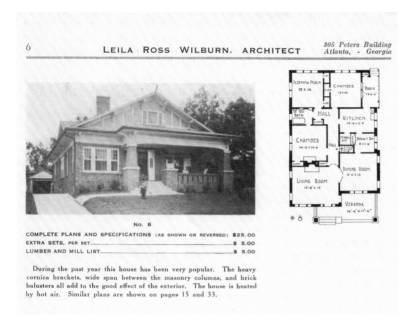

FIGURE 2.22. Plan design no. 8 in *Brick and Colonial Homes* offered a spacious, six-room, brick bungalow that became the most popular plan design in Wilburn's second plan book. The wide roof overhangs, brackets, large veranda, and grouped windows were among the prominent craftsman details.

the mail-order house plan from the plan book, and Figure 2.23 is a photograph of the plan book house built on Clifton Road in the Candler Park neighborhood in Atlanta.

In her next plan book, *Ideal Homes of Today*, Wilburn offered a smaller version of plan design no. 8, as shown in Figure 2.24: "A house similar to the one here shown was the most popular design in my book, '*Brick and Colonial Homes.*' . . . I have designed this house to give the same outside appearance, but have cut down the floor space about one-fifth. The room arrangement is practically the same, but the rooms are just a little smaller."[32] As Wilburn explained, the two house designs are practically

FIGURE 2.23. This craftsman bungalow, built in the Candler Park neighborhood in Atlanta, is an outstanding example of a house built from plan design no. 8. Many plan book houses were built in Atlanta area neighborhoods from this popular bungalow design. The location of the porch steps often varied from the plan design. Sometimes they were built on the side of the house closest to the driveway instead of in the front of the house, as shown in this photograph.

identical, with the later house, plan design no. 208, being a reduced floor plan and overall smaller bungalow design. Interestingly, the larger house, plan design no. 8, had two large chambers (bedrooms) with a large sleeping porch. The smaller house design had three smaller bedrooms and no sleeping porch. Other rooms common to both houses included a kitchen, breakfast room, dining room, living room, and hall bath. The veranda is designed as a large, open front porch in both plans, with front steps to the main entrance and a spacious sitting area located on the front corner of the house. Both plan book houses are shown with brick exteriors, stuccoed gable ends, and heavy brackets at the overhanging roof eaves. A house built on Cumberland Road in Atlanta from plan design no. 208 and its beautifully crafted front entrance are shown in Figures 2.25 and 2.26.

Although the bungalow for a time was one of the most dominant house types, representing "a better class of small domestic architecture," its popularity was short-lived.[33] As mentioned previously, the second wave of the eclectic period in American residential design took hold by the 1920s, when European-inspired historical styles reclaimed their popularity with American homeowners. Architectural styles such as colonial revival, neoclassical, Tudor, Italian, and Spanish revival were then used to create "period houses," which were built in suburbs throughout the country. The major shift to European-inspired "period houses" in the 1920s represents the second phase in the eclectic period, from 1920 to 1940.[34] According to McAlester, this shift in popular styles can be attributed to two significant historical developments. First, improvements in printing technologies made the cost of publishing much cheaper, and the era saw a wide distribution of many publications about architecture, from newspapers and magazines to books and reference materials. Architectural references and historical sources thus became more widely understood by both professionals and homeowners. Second, the development of masonry veneer construction reduced the construction costs of residential construction. As a consequence, historical, period houses in masonry became much

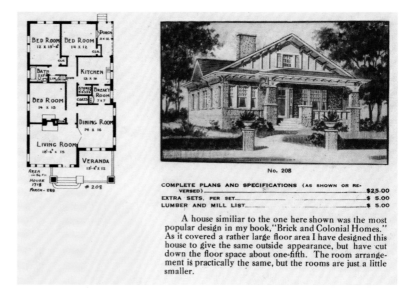

FIGURE 2.24. This bungalow design, no. 208, is a smaller version of plan design no. 8, with smaller rooms and a more compact floor plan. It was offered in Wilburn's third plan book as a more economical plan, following the popularity of the larger design in her second plan book. The two houses featured similar exterior craftsman-style details, including a spacious veranda used as an outdoor living space.

cheaper to build and, therefore, more affordable for the middle class.[35] As McAlester explained: "The new affordability of 'masonry' houses revolutionized the design of small homes. Previously, it had been difficult to copy historic European styles, as these were built of solid masonry, often with decorative stone- or brickwork patterns. Now, masonry veneers allowed modest cottages to mimic Old World dwellings."[36] Because a load-bearing masonry wall for exterior structure was no longer necessary, houses could be framed in wood, with non-load-bearing masonry veneer attached to the wood structure. This major development in building

FIGURE 2.25. This craftsman bungalow built on Cumberland Road in the Morningside neighborhood in Atlanta is an outstanding example of a smaller bungalow plan. Similar to plan design no. 8 (shown in Fig. 2.22), plan design 208 was smaller, with a more compact floor plan. Wilburn's interest in providing homeowners with design options in choosing an appropriate and affordable house plan can be seen in comparing plan design no. 8 and plan design no. 208.

FIGURE 2.26. The front entrance to the house on Cumberland Road built from plan design no. 208 included wide steps, a simple porch railing, brick columns, and a craftsman-style door with sidelights.

technology significantly reduced the cost of construction of these period houses, making them more affordable for middle-income households.

Beginning in the 1920s, Wilburn's plan designs reflected these changes in the American home. Her mail-order house plans shifted from offering primarily plain, post-Victorian southern homes and bungalows in her first plan book to more plan designs in the increasingly popular, European-inspired architectural styles. Beginning with her second plan book, Wilburn offered more house plans in these eclectic architectural styles with a variety of house sizes and plan arrangements in her four plan books published from 1921 (*Brick and Colonial Homes*) until ca. 1930 (*New Homes of Quality*).

In designing period houses, Wilburn often incorporated details, finishes, materials, and architectural features from more than one style, which was a typical practice in the early eclectic period. In later 1930s designs, rather than duplicating a particular historical style, architects loosely interpreted or adapted European traditions.[37] The American-style period home as such became an adaptive response to popular trends and middle-class needs, integrating early modern principles of efficiency, comfort, and simplicity with added historical features and details that provided scale and character but did not try to replicate exactly a particular historical style.

During the eclectic period, the English Tudor revival style, characterized by half-timber cladding, tall, vertical windows, and a massive chimney, was one of the most popular historical house styles. Loosely based on English architectural traditions, houses known as English Tudor revival or English vernacular revival often featured a side gable structure with front-facing gables, steeply pitched roofs, and a front door with a round arch, offering a picturesque style in affordable masonry veneer construction.[38] Wilburn's fourth plan book, *Homes in Good Taste*, offered many plan book houses in this eclectic historical style, including plan design no. 6255, shown in Figure 2.27. Wilburn described this plan as follows:

The charm of this English cottage is due to its steeply pitched roof and the attractive combination of brick, half-timber work and slate roof. The port cochere is convenient. The room arrangement is most compact, the area covered being far less than one would expect for seven main rooms, two baths, breakfast and sewing room. The living room fireplace is supplemented by a steam heating plant in the basement. The first story ceiling is 9 feet, while the second story has a full height of 8 feet, except for about one foot where the ceiling follows the line of the rafters.[39]

The Tudor revival features of this English cottage included a brick exterior with stucco and half-timber work in the gable ends, a front cross gable (living room), and a steeply pitched slate roof. The porte cochere, a covered drive-through space for automobiles on the side of the house, provided a porch connection from the car to the front entrance. The porte cochere was a popular feature from the 1920s to the 1930s, when garages typically were located behind the residence. As the predecessor to the carport and attached garage, the porte cochere is indicative of the growing presence and influence of the automobile in the design of the American home.

Plan design no. 6352, as shown in Figure 2.28, is another example of a Tudor revival–style English cottage. It was offered as a six-room house in *Homes in Good Taste*. Wilburn described this elegant plan design as follows:

A small house, even when built of the most simple materials, if properly designed, may be a thing of beauty. This also at no increased cost over a more commonplace type. The unusual design of the front chimney, the limestone-trimmed entrance the half-timber work in the gables, as well as the roof lines, add to the attractiveness of this compact, six-room English house. The design is of the front dining room type, giving privacy to the bed rooms. The breakfast room, many closets, ironing board, two corner bed rooms and hot air furnace will be appreciated.[40]

For a small, three-bedroom house, the prominent cross gabled front porch, brick exterior, limestone entry, front door with round arch, and massive

No. 6255

COMPLETE PLANS AND SPECIFICATIONS (AS SHOWN OR REVERSED) $30.00
EXTRA SETS, PER SET_____ $ 5.00
LUMBER AND MILL LIST_____ $ 5.00

The charm of this English cottage is due to its steeply pitched roof and the attractive combination of brick, half-timber work and slate roof. The porte cochere is convenient. The room arrangement is most compact, the area covered being far less than one would expect for seven main rooms, two baths, breakfast and sewing room. The living room fireplace is supplemented by a steam heating plant in the basement. The first story ceiling is 9 feet, while the second story has a full height of 8 feet, except for about one foot where the ceiling follows the line of rafters.

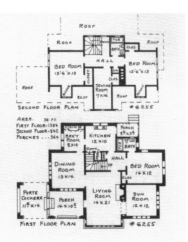

Order Plans From
LEILA ROSS WILBURN,
ARCHITECT
Peters Building, Atlanta, Ga.

FIGURE 2.27. Plan design no. 6255 in *Homes in Good Taste* offered a beautiful English cottage design with half-timber work, grouped windows, a slate roof, and a brick exterior. The downstairs bedroom and bath and large living room connected to a sunroom were among its distinguishing features. On the second level, the sewing room provided a convenient, personal workspace.

COMPLETE PLANS AND SPECIFICATIONS
(AS SHOWN OR REVERSED)____$20.00
EXTRA SETS, PER SET_____ $ 5.00
LUMBER AND MILL LIST_____ $ 5.00

No. 6352

Order Plans From
LEILA ROSS WILBURN,
ARCHITECT
Peters Building, Atlanta, Ga.

A small house, even when built of the most simple materials, if properly designed, may be a thing of beauty. This also at no increased cost over a more commonplace type. The unusual design of the front chimney, the limestone-trimmed entrance, the half-timber work in the gables, as well as the roof lines, add to the attractiveness of this compact, six-room English house. The design is of the front dining room type, giving privacy to the bed rooms. The breakfast room, many closets, ironing board, two corner bed rooms and hot air furnace will be appreciated.

FIGURE 2.28. Plan design no. 6352 in *Homes in Good Taste* was a six-room, one-story English-inspired cottage. This design is an example of a small period house that could be built affordably using masonry veneer construction. The half-timber work in the cross-gable front porch, limestone surround at the front door, wood door with round arch, grouped windows, and front chimney were among the details that provided architectural character and style.

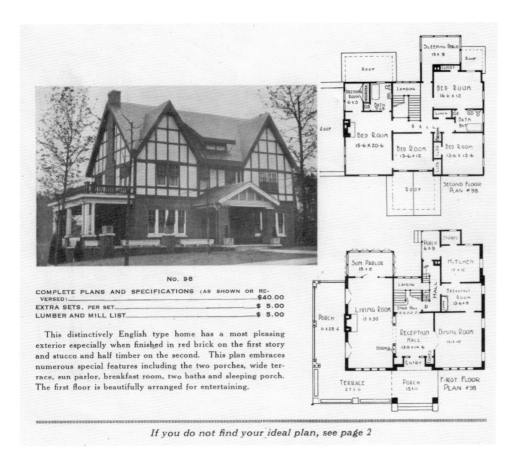

NO. 98

COMPLETE PLANS AND SPECIFICATIONS (AS SHOWN OR RE-
VERSED) _____ $40.00
EXTRA SETS, PER SET _____ $ 5.00
LUMBER AND MILL LIST _____ $ 5.00

This distinctively English type home has a most pleasing
exterior especially when finished in red brick on the first story
and stucco and half timber on the second. This plan embraces
numerous special features including the two porches, wide terrace, sun parlor, breakfast room, two baths and sleeping porch.
The first floor is beautifully arranged for entertaining.

If you do not find your ideal plan, see page 2

FIGURE 2.30. Built from plan design no. 98 on Fairview Road
in the Druid Hills neighborhood in Atlanta, this English,
Tudor revival–style house features half-timber work, prominent
front gables, and masonry veneer construction. The design is
one of the grandest examples of the English style period house
offered in Wilburn's early plan books.

FIGURE 2.29. The English Tudor revival–style home offered in plan design
no. 98 had a formal reception hall with a large living room, sun parlor,
dining room, breakfast room, and kitchen on the main level, and four
bedrooms, two baths, and a sleeping porch on the second level. The diversity
in size and plan arrangement for the English vernacular–style plan design can
be seen by comparing this design with the smaller English cottages shown in
Figures 2.27 and 2.28.

chimney created a beautifully designed exterior. As shown in Figure 2.28, the interior plan arrangement offered efficiency, comfort, and convenience, with modern heating, built-in storage, and large living spaces.

During the eclectic period, Tudor revival was a popular historical style not only for one-story house designs but also for larger, two-story houses. Wilburn offered a variety of Tudor revival plan designs in her early plan books, particularly her fourth and fifth plan books. The two-and-a-half-story Tudor revival house shown in Figure 2.29, plan design no. 98, was built on Fairview Road in the Druid Hills neighborhood in Atlanta and was one of the largest mail-order house plans offered in Wilburn's second plan book (see Fig. 2.30). Wilburn described the plan as follows: "This distinctively English type home has a most pleasing exterior especially when finished in red brick on the first story and stucco and half timber on the second. This plan embraces numerous special features including the two porches, wide terrace, sun parlor, breakfast room, two baths and sleeping porch. The first floor is beautifully arranged for entertaining."[41] The covered front porch entrance to this house connected an open terrace that extended across the front of the left side of the house to an open side porch. The light-filled living room spanned the width of the house, with French doors leading to the side porch and an enclosed sun parlor in the rear.

To the right of the reception hall, the large formal dining room in the front of the house was connected to a breakfast room with a large kitchen, pantry, and back porch extending to the rear of the house. The symmetrically placed front entrance to the home opened into a reception hall with connections to the living room on the left and the dining room to the right of the entrance. Beyond the reception hall, a large stair hall and a grand staircase led to four large bedrooms, two baths, spacious closets, and a sleeping porch on the second level. A master bedroom above the 15-by-30-foot living room included a walk-in dressing room with built-in wardrobe and a large bath. It was one of the earliest examples of a master suite offered in Wilburn's plan book designs.

Another large two-story house from Wilburn's second plan book, plan design no. 64, is shown in Figure 2.31. Houses from this plan design were built in the Druid Hills neighborhood in Atlanta on Springdale Road (Fig. 2.32) and on Fairview Road (Fig. 2.33). Each house was adapted to fit its building site in specific ways. The house on Springdale Road was designed with a large lower level and a wide set of prominent porch steps leading to the covered entry. The house on Fairview Road, however, was designed with the front entrance at grade. As shown in Figures 2.32 and 2.33, the house design featured a prominent covered entry, with large brackets supporting a roof structure. Wilburn used variations of this design feature, with different brackets and roof structures, on many of her southern homes. She described this plan book house as follows: "The hooded entrance and large side veranda, shown here, is often desired. Attention should center on such features as the large living room, sun parlor, breakfast room, and two baths."[42] The large closets, including a trunk room, the sleeping porch, sun parlor, veranda, and spacious living areas are other attractive features in this house design. This plan design had many of the same interior spaces as the Tudor revival–style house shown in Figure 2.30. The veranda was designed as an open side porch directly connected to the large living room by French doors. The second level had three bedrooms, two baths, and a sleeping porch, with a number of closets, including a large trunk room and linen closet off the main hall. Large windows on both levels provided an abundance of fresh air and daylight. On the exterior, colonial revival features included a prominent front door, sidelights, and double hung windows. Wooden benches on either side of the front door, a flower box on the second level, and eyebrow dormers were simple architectural features that added scale and character to this brick home.

The colonial revival style was one of the most popular historical styles during the first half of the century. It was offered in all five of Wilburn's early plan books in one-story and two-story house designs. The colonial revival style featured a symmetrical façade and exterior architectural

No. 64

COMPLETE PLANS AND SPECIFICA-
TIONS (AS SHOWN OR REVERSED) $30.00
EXTRA SETS, PER SET _____ $ 5.00
LUMBER AND MILL LIST _____ $ 5.00

The hooded entrance and large side veranda, shown here, is often desired. Attention should center on such features as the large living room, sun parlor, breakfast room, and two baths.

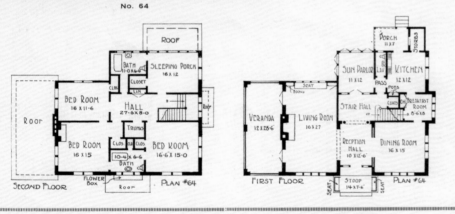

Carry the interior plastering to the floor, it makes a warmer house

FIGURE 2.31. Plan design no. 64 in *Brick and Colonial Homes* offered a floor plan that was similar but smaller than plan design no. 98 in a colonial revival–style design. The prominent architectural features included a symmetrical façade, double-hung windows, and side lights at the front entrance. The hooded front entrance supported by large wooden brackets was a common feature on many of Wilburn's plan book houses in this popular style.

FIGURE 2.32. This home was built on Springdale Road in the Druid Hills neighborhood in Atlanta from plan design no. 64. It varies from the original plan book design in having a large basement and stone foundation with a wide set of stairs leading to the first level.

FIGURE 2.33. This home was built on Fairview Road in the Druid Hills neighborhood in Atlanta from plan design no. 64. In a variation from the plan book design, the eyebrow dormers on the front elevation are larger and are located above the second level windows.

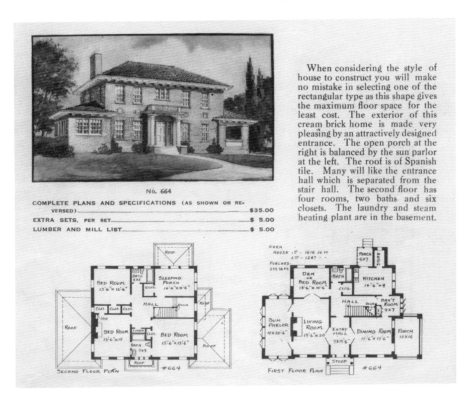

No. 664

COMPLETE PLANS AND SPECIFICATIONS (AS SHOWN OR RE-
    VERSED) _____ $35.00
EXTRA SETS, PER SET _____ $ 5.00
LUMBER AND MILL LIST _____ $ 5.00

When considering the style of
house to construct you will make
no mistake in selecting one of the
rectangular type as this shape gives
the maximum floor space for the
least cost. The exterior of this
cream brick home is made very
pleasing by an attractively designed
entrance. The open porch at the
right is balanced by the sun parlor
at the left. The roof is of Spanish
tile. Many will like the entrance
hall which is separated from the
stair hall. The second floor has
four rooms, two baths and six
closets. The laundry and steam
heating plant are in the basement.

FIGURE 2.34. Plan design no. 664 featured an elegant design for a two-story colonial revival–style home. The spacious floor plan offered convenience, comfort, flexibility, and efficiency in a simple plan arrangement. Attractive interior spaces included a large sun parlor connected to the living room and a flexible den/bedroom space on the first level.

details that included prominent porch columns, boxed cornices, double hung windows, and a prominent front door with an overhead fanlight and side lights. Many colonial revival–style houses were also built with a cross gable front porch with columns.[43]

A notable example of a two-story colonial revival house in Wilburn's third plan book, plan design no. 664, had a symmetrical façade, side lights, front columns, decorative railing above the front entrance, and double hung windows, with a green tile roof that suggested a Mediterranean influence. The rectilinear floor plan provided spacious living spaces and light-filled interiors in a simple plan arrangement (see Fig. 2.34). Wilburn described the design as follows:

When considering the style of house to construct you will make no mistake in selecting one of the rectangular type as this shape gives the maximum floor space for the least cost. The exterior of this cream brick home is made very pleasing by an attractively designed entrance. The open porch at the right is balanced by the sun parlor at the left. The roof is of Spanish tile. Many will like the entrance hall which is separated from the stair hall. The second floor has four rooms, two baths and six closets. The laundry and steam heating plant are in the basement.[44]

The spacious, nine-room house included a formal entry hall that separated the living and dining spaces. The living room was flanked by a large sun parlor on one side of the front entrance; the dining room had a direct

FIGURE 2.35. This attractive colonial revival house was built on North Decatur Road in the Druid Hills neighborhood in Atlanta from plan design no. 664. With simple massing and a brick exterior, the house had a symmetrical façade with a sun parlor balanced by an open porch on each end of the front elevation.

connection to the side porch that provided balance and symmetry on the front elevation. Beyond the living room on the rear of the house, adjacent to the bath and opposite the kitchen was a den that also could serve as a downstairs bedroom. The upstairs featured three large bedrooms and a sleeping porch. This house is one of the grander homes in Wilburn's third plan book, an elegant design that was built on North Decatur Road in the Druid Hills neighborhood in Atlanta (see Fig. 2.35).

As previous examples have shown, Wilburn offered a variety of different designs for porches intended to be used as functional, outdoor areas. Many colonial revival houses, instead of featuring a prominent front porch, were designed with a cross gable porch, with a side porch serving as an informal social space and sitting area. Often referred to as a "living porch," the side porch, with direct connections to the living room, served as an adjacent outdoor living space in many of Wilburn's plan designs. Plan design no. 303 in Wilburn's third plan book, as shown in Figure 2.36, was a colonial revival house that featured a large living room with a door to a large side porch. Wilburn described this plan as follows:

> Of typical American design, there is a distinct charm to this red brick house with this green tile roof that kindles the desire to "Own Your Own Home." The room arrangement is good and those on the first floor open up to give a spacious effect. The stair is particularly attractive. The sun room could be used for a bed room as there is a lavatory accessible on the

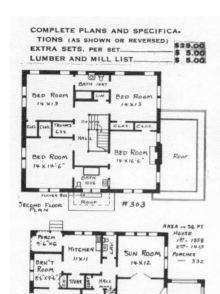

No. 303

Of typical American design, there is a distinct charm to this red brick house with this green tile roof that kindles the desire to "Own Your Own Home." The room arrangement is good and those on the first floor open up to give a spacious effect. The stair is particularly attractive. The sun room could be used for a bed room as there is a lavatory accessible on the first floor. The second floor rooms have four windows each, fine closets and direct bath connection.

FIGURE 2.36. Plan design no. 303 is another example of a period house designed in the colonial revival style. It offered spacious living areas with an open staircase in the central hall and a typical four-bedroom, two-bath plan on the second level.

first floor. The second floor rooms have four windows each, fine closets, and direct bath connection.[45]

This plan design was built in the Druid Hills neighborhood in Atlanta, as shown in Figure 2.37. This two-story house has a symmetrical façade with a prominent gabled entry and large windows on both levels. The floor plan resembled many of Wilburn's early southern homes, with large living spaces connected by French doors on the first level and four corner bedrooms and connecting baths on the second level.

Ideal Homes of Today, Wilburn's third plan book, offered a number of two-story, eclectic style houses as mail-order house plans. Built in the

Druid Hills neighborhood in Atlanta, plan design no. 1003, shown in Figure 2.38, was designed as a large, two-story brick residence, rectangular in form, with a tile roof, a front terrace, and a prominent, columned entrance. The wood trellis work surrounding the living room windows on the first level and the window railings provided simple, beautiful details for the front façade, as shown in Figure 2.39. The large entrance hall opened into the living room that extended across the front of the house and was connected to the adjacent sun room and the formal dining room on the back of the house. The living room, sun room, and dining room opened up spatially and visually to provide light-filled living spaces

FIGURE 2.37. This attractive two-story colonial revival home was built on North Decatur Road in the Druid Hills neighborhood in Atlanta from plan design no. 303. Like many other plan book designs in this style, it featured a two-story façade with a one-story side porch that offered a large outdoor living space directly connected to the living room.

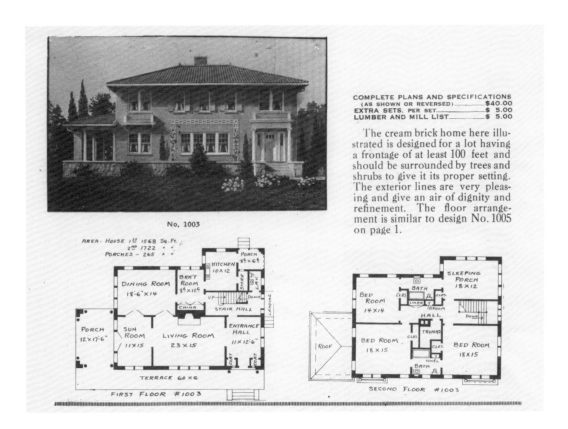

COMPLETE PLANS AND SPECIFICATIONS
(AS SHOWN OR REVERSED)_____$40.00
EXTRA SETS, PER SET_____$ 5.00
LUMBER AND MILL LIST_____$ 5.00

The cream brick home here illustrated is designed for a lot having a frontage of at least 100 feet and should be surrounded by trees and shrubs to give it its proper setting. The exterior lines are very pleasing and give an air of dignity and refinement. The floor arrangement is similar to design No. 1005 on page 1.

No. 1003

AREA-HOUSE 1ST 1568 Sq. Ft.
2ND 1722 " "
PORCHES - 265 " "

FIRST FLOOR #1003

SECOND FLOOR #1003

FIGURE 2.38. Plan design no. 1003 offered a colonial revival–style home with a rectangular plan for a lot with wide frontage, allowing the entrance hall, living room, sunroom, and side porch to face the street. The dining, breakfast, and kitchen spaces faced the back yard. The second level included three spacious bedrooms, two baths, a large trunk room, and a sleeping porch.

on the first level. The second level was a typical southern home floor plan with large corner bedrooms, a sleeping porch in the rear, direct bath connections, and a number of storage closets, including a trunk room off the main hall. The spacious room sizes and plan arrangement have offered comfortable accommodations and flexible interior spaces through the years to several generations of homeowners, allowing flexibility and adaptation, with few changes to the original floor plan.

Another colonial revival–style house offered in *Brick and Colonial Homes*, plan design no. 137, is a beautiful example of the simplicity and elegance offered by eclectic period house designs: "Another delightful Colonial house, much thought of by those who prefer simple dignity in home architecture. This house has a certain richness of proportions and details, relieved of any forms of ostentation, and an entire absence of objectionable qualities. The cream brick, white trim, and Spanish tile roof are typical of this design. The first floor arrangement is admirable, and the bed rooms are very conveniently arranged as to baths and closets."[46] The notable colonial revival features for this house design included a prominent front door with a simple columned entrance, double-hung windows, and a symmetrical façade (see Fig. 2.40). As with many of Wilburn's colonial revival plan book houses, its two-story symmetrical

FIGURE 2.39. This colonial revival–style home was built on North Decatur Road in the Druid Hills neighborhood in Atlanta from plan design no. 1003. The wood trellis work, window railing, elevated terrace, and front entrance are exterior features that provide scale and character to the simple massing and brick exterior of this attractive home.

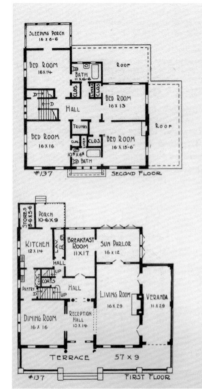

No. 137

COMPLETE PLANS AND SPECIFICATIONS (AS SHOWN OR REVERSED) $35.00
EXTRA SETS, PER SET_____ $ 5.00
LUMBER AND MILL LIST_____ $ 5.00

Another delightful Colonial house, much thought of by those who prefer simple dignity in home architecture. This house has a certain richness of proportions and details, relieved of any forms of ostentation, and an entire absence of objectionable qualities. The cream brick, white trim, and Spanish tile roof are typical of this design. The first floor arrangement is admirable, and the bed rooms are very conveniently arranged as to baths and closets.

FIGURE 2.40. A colonial revival–style home, plan design no. 137 featured a spacious floor plan that was typical of many of Wilburn's plan book houses in this style. The first level included a large reception hall, which connected the dining and living room spaces across the front of the house. Pocket doors, French doors, and cased openings connected the living spaces, which could be opened up for entertaining.

façade was offset by a one-story side porch. With a direct connection to the front terrace and living room, the side porch functioned as a convenient outdoor living room. Spacious living spaces on the first level included a large reception hall, a dining room, a living room, and a sun parlor, which were connected by pocket doors, French doors, and wide, cased openings. The second-level spaces included four large bedrooms, a sleeping porch, two baths, and a trunk room. The house shown in Figure 2.41 was built from this plan on Springdale Road in the Druid Hills neighborhood in Atlanta.

Although two-story houses were popular with homeowners and contractors in newly developed suburbs and neighborhoods, Wilburn also offered a variety of smaller, one-story plan book houses, typically five-room or six-room designs, in a range of architectural styles. Plan design no. 135 is an outstanding example of a small, popular one-story house from Wilburn's second plan book, shown in Figure 2.42. This charming house featured a wood trellis design on the screened porch and was offered in a five- or six-room plan in frame or wood construction. Wilburn described this plan as follows: "Many have admired this little brick bungalow,

FIGURE 2.41. This period house was built on Springdale Road in the Druid Hills neighborhood in Atlanta from plan design no. 137. It is another outstanding example of a colonial revival–style plan book house, similar to others shown in Wilburn's second and third plan books. Finely crafted architectural features and details included wood shutters, second-level window boxes, a terrace balustrade, and a columned entrance.

NO. 135 AND NO. 135-B

COMPLETE PLANS AND SPECIFICATIONS (AS SHOWN OR RE-
VERSED)_____$20.00
EXTRA SETS, PER SET_____$ 5.00
LUMBER AND MILL LIST_____$ 5.00

Many have admired this little brick bungalow, therefore I am
offering it with either five or six rooms. The simple straightforward
lines are relieved by the circular hood and porch trellis work. Two
fireplaces supplement the warm air furnace. The breakfast room
will make the house work lighter. See page 21 for a larger similar
design. I can also furnish these plans for frame construction.

FIGURE 2.43. This house was built on *Ponce de Leon Place* in the *Ponce de Leon Terrace* neighborhood in Decatur, Ga., from plan design no. 135. The arched, hooded entrance supported by brackets, the grouped windows, the vertical diamond trellis work, and the side porch are among the finely crafted details on this attractive brick bungalow.

FIGURE 2.42. Plan design no. 135 and no. 135-B offered a charming colonial revival–style bungalow with two floor plan options, either a two-bedroom or a three bedroom design. The compact floor plans included a breakfast room, closet spaces, and central heating, which offered convenience and comfort in these small house designs.

therefore I am offering it with either five or six rooms. The simple straightforward lines are relieved by the circular hood and porch trellis work. Two fireplaces supplement the warm air furnace. The breakfast room will make the house work lighter."[47] A house built from plan no. 135, shown in Figure 2.43, is on Ponce de Leon Place in the historic Ponce de Leon Terrace neighborhood, a subdivision developed in Decatur in 1913. Figure 2.44 shows a house built as a reverse plan of no. 135 on Lindbergh Drive in Atlanta. Figure 2.45 shows a wooden, vertical diamond trellis design on the screened porch on the house on Lindbergh Drive.

FIGURE 2.44. This house was built on Lindbergh Drive in Atlanta from a reverse plan of plan design no. 135. The vertical diamond trellis work and the slate roof are among the picturesque details on this attractive brick bungalow.

FIGURE 2.45. This vertical diamond trellis work, shown in plan design no. 135, was a common architectural feature on many one-story homes in Wilburn's early plan books. The trellis was constructed from stock lumber and typically painted white to match the exterior woodwork.

Plan design no. 24 is another beautiful example of a one-story plan book house in the colonial revival style (see Fig. 2.46). Published in *Brick and Colonial Homes*, the design featured a large one-story home with spacious rooms, including a living room and music room connected by French doors across the front half of the house. A kitchen, a built-in breakfast area, a dining room, three bedrooms, a large sleeping porch, and an abundance of storage spaces made this a very livable southern home. Figure 2.47 shows a house built on Springdale Road in the Druid Hills neighborhood in Atlanta from this plan design. A large veranda with a cross gable roof provided a prominent outdoor living space. The porte cochere offered a convenient, covered area from the front door to the vehicular drive through area. On the exterior, the foundation, the porte cochere, and the porch columns were brick construction. The house had wide roof overhangs with large wooden brackets, a typical feature of many bungalow designs. Colonial revival–style features included side lights at the front entry and Palladian windows in the dormer and gable end of the front porch, as shown in Figure 2.48.

Plan design no. 503, a charming one-story, colonial revival brick cottage, had a symmetrical façade with a prominent front porch. The porch is framed with double (wood) columns, boxed eaves, and a fan motif in the projecting, cross gable end. The vertical, diamond wood trellis featured on the corners of the house provided a handcrafted, decorative element on the front façade. Wilburn published this six-room plan design in *Ideal Homes of Today*. The living room was connected to the den and dining rooms by large openings with French doors. Built-in features included a china cabinet in the breakfast room, linen and coat closets in the back hall, and bookcases on either size of the fireplace in the living room, as shown in Figure 2.49. Examples of houses built from plan design no. 503 in the Candler Park neighborhood in Atlanta are shown in Figures 2.50 and 2.51.

The house styles in *Homes in Good Taste* offered a wide range of popular architectural styles from the eclectic period in American residential

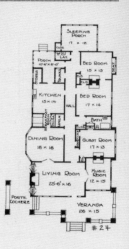

NO. 24

COMPLETE PLANS AND SPECIFICATIONS (AS SHOWN OR REVERSED) $25.00
EXTRA SETS. PER SET_____ $ 5.00
LUMBER AND MILL LIST_____ $ 5.00

To one needing a large house and desiring the rooms all on one floor
this home should appeal. The two baths, breakfast room, and porte
cochere are added features. The outside walls are of 10-inch white
boards, foundation and chimneys of cream brick, and roof of green
asphalt shingles. A similar front is found on page 24 in a story and a
half design.

FIGURE 2.46. Plan design no. 24 was a large colonial style brick
bungalow offered in Wilburn's second plan book. The compact
bungalow floor plan was expanded to provide spacious interiors,
including a living, dining, and music room (connected by
French doors), with three bedrooms, two baths, and a sleeping
porch. Built-in furnishings included breakfast-room seating, a
china cabinet, a window seat in a bedroom, and bookcases in
the living room.

FIGURE 2.47. This house was built on Springdale Road in the Druid Hills
neighborhood in Atlanta from plan design no. 24. The cross-gabled veranda, red
tile roof, wood roof brackets, and Palladian windows are among the charming
architectural features and details on this attractive brick home.

FIGURE 2.48. The
gabled dormer on
plan design no. 24 is
a beautifully designed
architectural feature
with a tile roof, wide
roof overhangs,
exposed rafters,
wood brackets, and a
Palladian window.

No. 503

FIGURE 2.49. Plan design no. 503 offered a colonial revival–style brick bungalow in a seven-room floor plan that included a den, living room, and dining room connected by French doors. The two-bedroom design was a typical bungalow plan with a breakfast room that offered a convenient, informal eating area between the kitchen and dining room.

FIGURE 2.50. This house was built on McLendon Avenue in the Candler Park neighborhood in Atlanta from plan design no. 503. The symmetrical façade with a large cross-gabled front porch, the fan motif in the gable end, boxed eaves, and double columns were among the colonial revival–style features on this brick bungalow.

FIGURE 2.51. This house was built on McLendon Avenue in the Candler Park neighborhood in Atlanta from plan design no. 503. It is located on the opposite corner from an identical house built from the same plan book design shown in FIGURE 2.50. In addition to the colonial revival features, each plan book house has a vertical diamond trellis on each end of the front elevation, which is original to the plan design (as shown in Fig. 2.49).

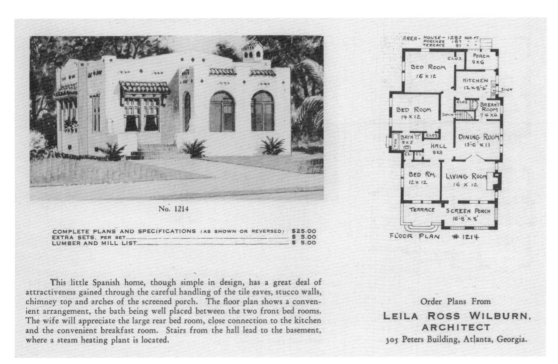

No. 1214

COMPLETE PLANS AND SPECIFICATIONS (AS SHOWN OR REVERSED) $25.00
EXTRA SETS, PER SET_____ $ 5.00
LUMBER AND MILL LIST_____ $ 5.00

This little Spanish home, though simple in design, has a great deal of
attractiveness gained through the careful handling of the tile eaves, stucco walls,
chimney top and arches of the screened porch. The floor plan shows a convenient arrangement, the bath being well placed between the two front bed rooms.
The wife will appreciate the large rear bed room, close connection to the kitchen
and the convenient breakfast room. Stairs from the hall lead to the basement,
where a steam heating plant is located.

Order Plans From
Leila Ross Wilburn,
ARCHITECT
305 Peters Building, Atlanta, Georgia.

FIGURE 2.52. Plan design no. 1214 is one of the few Spanish revival–style designs offered as a mail-order house plan in Wilburn's early plan books. It reflects the popularity of the eclectic period houses during the 1920s and 1930s. The three-bedroom plan design included a typical bungalow floor plan.

design. As Wilburn stated in this plan book: "Here are 53 designs in the latest styles; homes derived from the English cottage, French farmhouse, Italian villa, and our own early American Colonial. More and more modern homes are showing the influence of old world architecture."[48]

Plan design no. 1214 is an outstanding example of Wilburn's dexterity in creating a beautiful home with a European-inspired exterior and an efficient and spacious floor plan (see Fig. 2.52). In describing this house, Wilburn wrote: "This little Spanish home, though simple in design, has a great deal of attractiveness gained through the careful handling of the tile eaves, stucco walls, chimney top and arches of the screened porch. The floor plan shows a convenient arrangement, the bath being well placed between the two front bed rooms. The wife will appreciate the large rear bed room, close connection to the kitchen, and the convenient breakfast room."[49] The reverse plan (which Wilburn offered as a stock plan upon request at no additional cost) was built in Athens, Georgia, in 1927 and underwent extensive restoration and expansion in 2014–2016 (see Fig. 2.53). This house is featured in Chapter 4 as an example of a plan book house that has undergone extensive renovation, retaining its historic character while adapting to the needs of its owners in the twenty-first century (see pp. 117–119).

Few complete copies of Wilburn's fifth plan book, *New Homes of Quality*, survive, but some loose pages held in the collections of the Atlanta History Center include many English vernacular revival–style plan designs, which were characterized by brick veneer exteriors, steeply

FIGURE 2.53. This house was built on Cobb Street in Athens, Ga., from a reverse plan of plan design no. 1214. The stucco exterior, parapet roof, chimney cap with clay tile roof, and arched openings on the screened porch are among the architectural features that were characteristic of the Spanish revival style.

pitched roofs, sweeping, curved front gables, and arches at the front door or porch area, with half-timber and stone trim.[50] Many of these houses featured a one-and-a-half-story plan with a permanent, enclosed stair to an attic space. The unfinished second-level space provided flexibility and economy in allowing homeowners to use the space as storage or complete it later as additional bedrooms and baths.

Wilburn described plan design no. 2054, shown in Figure 2.54, as a "purely American home." This phrase seems to refer to the combination of the Tudor revival style with the compact, modern floor plan, convenient plan arrangement, and attractive interiors—an adaption of European style to modern life as a uniquely American style. Plan design no. 2054 is an example of how period houses were designed for efficiency, convenience, and economy with exteriors that reflected popular eclectic style houses. Her description of it read as follows:

This purely American home has features that take it out of the commonplace. The walls are of red brick, entrance of tan stone, trim painted a rich cream color, and roof in blended shades of green, gray and red asphalt shingles. The splendid arrangement of the six rooms is to be noted. The living room, with its bay window, being a most attractive room. Plaster arches connect living room, entrance hall and dining room. The breakfast room, with its corner cupboards, adds to the vista across the front of the house. The kitchen has double windows over the sink, and the cabinets at the side are so arranged that all work may be easily performed. The bedrooms are closely connected with the two baths. In the attic there is height

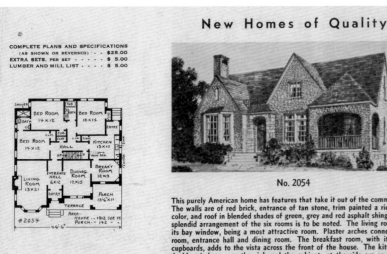

COMPLETE PLANS AND SPECIFICATIONS
(AS SHOWN OR REVERSED) - - $25.00
EXTRA SETS, PER SET - - - - $ 5.00
LUMBER AND MILL LIST - - - - $ 5.00

No. 2054

This purely American home has features that take it out of the commonplace. The walls are of red brick, entrance of tan stone, trim painted a rich cream color, and roof in blended shades of green, grey and red asphalt shingles. The splendid arrangement of the six rooms is to be noted. The living room, with its bay window, being a most attractive room. Plaster arches connect living room, entrance hall and dining room. The breakfast room, with its corner cupboards, adds to the vista across the front of the house. The kitchen has double windows over the sink and the cabinets at the side are so arranged that all work may be easily performed. The bedrooms are closely connected with the two baths. In the attic there is height for one or two rooms when needed. The basement takes care of the steam heating plant, laundry and a servant's toilet. A similar floor arrangement, without the entrance hall, is shown on page 16.

Order Plans From
LEILA ROSS WILBURN
ARCHITECT
305 Peters Building, Atlanta, Georgia

FIGURE 2.54. An attractive English-inspired period house, plan design no. 2054 was offered in *New Homes of Quality*, Wilburn's fifth plan book. It offered a compact floor plan in a one-and-a-half-story cottage design, with permanent stairs to attic space for storage or future expansion space.

for one or two rooms when needed. The basement takes care of the steam heating plant, laundry and a servant's toilet.[51]

This plan design, like many in Wilburn's plan books, provided a permanent staircase to an unfinished attic space that could be built out at a later date if expansion space was needed.

Throughout her career Wilburn demonstrated her agility in offering a diverse range of plan book designs that reflected the changing needs of homeowners as well as the latest trends in domestic architecture. In offering mail-order house plans, Wilburn recommended that homeowners

and builders select contextually appropriate designs. Although she presumably had no influence on where her plan book designs would be built, she believed that houses should fit the architectural context and natural environment and contribute in a positive way to the architectural character and scale of their surroundings. In the foreword to her second plan book, *Brick and Colonial Homes*, Wilburn wrote:

> The building of a home is an important event in any life. That's the best reason you can find for planning carefully every feature of your house. Some say, "Never mind the exterior, I live inside—not outside. Give me a beautiful interior and my neighbors will have to put up with the outside." This is not right. We owe something to our neighbors; we do care what they think of the appearance of our home, and the ideal home is a well-balanced structure, harmonious in detail, and attractive outside as well as inside. Those houses which have that "indescribable something" are, after all, an expression of the owner's individuality.[52]

Figure 2.55 shows an attractive colonial revival–style plan design from Wilburn's fifth plan book, *New Homes of Quality*.

As shown throughout this chapter, Wilburn's early plan book houses, which Wilburn offered as modern American homes, had compact floor plans and were more uniform in exterior form, style, and appearance than their nineteenth-century predecessors. Incorporating new domestic technologies and offering more efficient living spaces, Wilburn's plan book houses reflected popular trends and shifting priorities in houses designs in the early twentieth century. In place of the highly decorative exterior and large, irregular floor plan of the Victorian house, popular house designs typically had smaller, more efficient floor plans and used stock building materials and standard building construction to create more economical designs and plainer exteriors. These house designs featured architectural details such as trellises, pergolas, and roof brackets as decorative elements with simpler designs that were constructed from stock lumber. Readily available building materials and stock building components from local companies and manufacturers, such as lumber, roofing, masonry, and millwork, offered efficiency and economy in the construction of the modern, progressive home.

Clifford Edward Clark Jr., in *The American Family Home*, described the shift in priorities and attitudes that led to the design of the modern American home as follows: "What started in the 1890s as an attempt to revise housing standards and family ideals became after 1900 a full-blown

FIGURE 2.55. Plan design no. 3856, one of the largest colonial revival–style houses from Wilburn's early plan books, was published in *New Homes of Quality*. It had many of the popular features that Wilburn used in other plan book designs, including a sun room connected to the living room, a porch connected to the dining room, and a library on the first level that could also function as a bedroom. The second level included four bedrooms and two baths, with a sewing room designed as a flexible living space.

crusade to demolish the older Victorian beliefs. . . . In place of an aesthetic which valued complexity and richness of design, they advocated a more spartan ethic. Houses should be simple, efficient, neat, and natural. The profile of the residence should be straight and clean. Whether the exterior favored Colonial Revival forms, the low horizontality of the Prairie School designs, or the simple outlines of the bungalow, the principles of design were the same: structural simplicity, balanced proportions, and minimal decoration."[53] Following this new modern aesthetic, Wilburn rarely used elaborate architectural details and instead created finely crafted architectural designs and decorative elements utilizing economical building materials, standard building components, and conventional framing. Simple architectural details such as wood trellises, window boxes, ornamental brackets, and hooded entrances added scale and architectural character to the exterior façade.

A beautiful, yet simple, exterior detail often seen on Wilburn's plan book houses is a vertical wooden trellis designed as a handcrafted, decorative element on a porch or front façade. The vertical diamond trellis design shown in Figure 2.56 was featured on plan design no. 135, one of Wilburn's smaller plan book houses (shown in Fig. 2.43). The house built as a reverse plan and shown in Figures 2.44 and 2.45 had a somewhat different diamond trellis design. Plan design no. 503, which was described earlier (see Figs. 2.50 and 2.51), included another attractive diamond trellis design constructed from stock lumber.

Other simple design details that were prevalent on Wilburn's plan book houses included oversized wooden brackets at roof eaves and at covered entrances, particularly for colonial revival and European-inspired house designs. On a house designed from the reverse plan of plan design no. 661, shown in Figure 2.57, the gabled entrance supported by large wooden brackets appears to float above the front door and covered entrance.

Wilburn also offered different options in exterior cladding materials for some of her mail-order plans. This was a practical design option as well as

FIGURE 2.56. This vertical diamond trellis design was a decorative architectural detail on the screened porch on plan design no. 135 in *Brick and Colonial Homes* (shown in Fig. 2.42). Built from stock lumber and typically painted white to match the exterior wood trim, the vertical diamond trellis was a decorative feature on many of Wilburn's smaller plan book houses.

FIGURE 2.57. As shown on this and other plan book houses, a hooded entrance supported by large wood brackets was a prevalent architectural feature on many of Wilburn's period houses. This particular design is shown on a house built from a reverse plan of plan design no. 661 on 17th Street in the Ansley Park neighborhood in Atlanta.

an important business strategy, as each material had particular characteristics as well as costs. In her second plan book, Wilburn explained the choices in exterior materials, describing the respective advantages of brick, stucco, and wood cladding. She began, "There is nothing which will give the house so much dignity, stability and permanence as brick," listing the lower insurance rates, thermal efficiency, and lower maintenance among the advantages of a brick exterior.[54] For the wood frame house, she explained that it "needs no introduction, it is suitable for many localities, can be made most attractive, and on account of the low cost is one of the most popular materials of which to build."[55]

House plan no. 660 in *Ideal Homes of Today*, shown in Figure 2.58, was used to build two houses in the Druid Hills neighborhood in Atlanta, one in brick and the other in wood frame construction. The house on Oakdale Road, shown in Figure 2.59, was constructed with a brick exterior and a clay tile roof. The house on Fairview Road, shown in Figure 2.60, was constructed with a wood exterior and an asphalt shingle roof. The front entrances, shown in Figure 2.61 for the Oakdale Road house and Figure 2.62 for the Fairview Road house, feature prominent hooded entrances with brackets supporting a covered entry for the front door. The colonial revival influences in the exterior design of plan design no. 660 included exterior columns on the side porch or veranda, window shutters, and a symmetrical façade. Wilburn described the house's features as follows:

> The Colonial influence is evident in this house through the use of white columns, wide siding and shuttered windows. The arched hood has sufficient projection to form a shelter for the front door. Those who dislike entering directly into the living room will appreciate the private entrance hall which connects the living room and dining room. The sun parlor may easily be used as a bed room, the stair hall connecting this room with the bath and service portion of the house.

The seven closets and direct bath connections make the second floor all that could be desired.[56]

The second level of this home is a typical one for a two-story southern home, with three large corner bedrooms, two baths, a sleeping porch, and storage closets for clothes and linens.

In addition to single-family residences, Wilburn included a number of designs for "two-family houses," which essentially were duplex designs, in each of her early plan books. This house type demonstrated Wilburn's interest in providing mail-order house plans for southerners needing economical and practical designs for a two-family residence.

These two-family houses were designed to offer diversity in dwelling for multi-family households as well as economical options for homeowners.[57]

In *Southern Homes and Bungalows*, plan no. 1142 was a "two-family apartment" with a separate apartment on each of two levels (see Fig. 2.63). Wilburn described this duplex design as follows: "This two-family apartment is shown, as it has the appearance of a private residence. The exterior walls are a dark brown stained siding, while the trim is painted white. The four rooms are arranged so that, by the use of 'In-a-Dor' folding beds, three of the rooms may be used as a living room, dining room, and den during the day and also as perfect bed rooms during the night. Each bed folds up into a closet that has a window in it."[58] This large, two-story

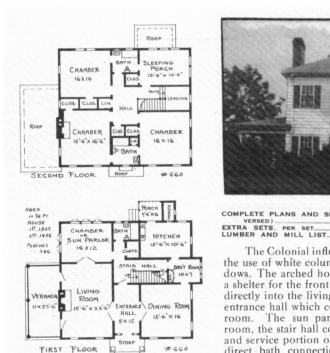

No. 660

COMPLETE PLANS AND SPECIFICATIONS (AS SHOWN OR RE-
VERSED) _____ $35.00
EXTRA SETS, PER SET_____ $ 5.00
LUMBER AND MILL LIST_____ $ 5.00

The Colonial influence is evident in this house through the use of white columns, wide siding and shuttered windows. The arched hood has sufficient projection to form a shelter for the front door. Those who dislike entering directly into the living room will appreciate the private entrance hall which connects the living room and dining room. The sun parlor may easily be used as a bed room, the stair hall connecting this room with the bath and service portion of the house. The seven closets and direct bath connection make the second floor all that could be desired.

FIGURE 2.58. Plan design no. 660 was a colonial revival–style period home with a symmetrical two-story façade and a one-story veranda on the front of the house. It offered many popular features, including a sun parlor that could be used as a downstairs bedroom and a large veranda connected to the living room.

FIGURE 2.59. This house was built with a brick exterior on Oakdale Road in the Druid Hills neighborhood in Atlanta from plan design no. 660. The symmetrical two-story façade, double-hung windows, boxed eaves, fan light, and side lights at the front entrance were among the distinguishing colonial revival features of this attractive home.

FIGURE 2.61. The front entrance to the brick home built from plan design no. 660 on Oakdale Road (shown in Fig. 2.59) included an arched hood with wooden brackets above the front door.

FIGURE 2.60. This house was built with a wood siding exterior and wood shutters on Fairview Road in the Druid Hills neighborhood in Atlanta from plan design no. 660. It had the same distinguishing colonial revival features as the home built in brick from the same plan design that is shown in FIGURE 2.59.

FIGURE 2.62. The front entrance for the home with wood siding built from plan design no. 660 on Fairview Road had the same colonial revival features and architectural details as the house shown and described in FIGURE 2.60.

Design No. 1142

THIS two-family apartment is shown, as it has the appearance of a private residence. The exterior walls are a dark brown stained siding, while the trim is painted white. The four rooms are arranged so that, by the use of "In-a-Dor" folding beds, three of the rooms may be used as living room, dining room and den during the day and also as perfect bed rooms during the night. Each bed folds up into a closet that has a window in it.

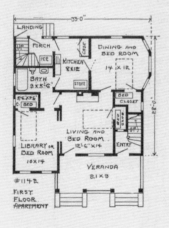

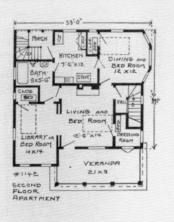

dwelling offered affordable, flexible accommodations as a two-family residence.

In her fourth plan book, *Homes in Good Taste*, Wilburn offered a two-story, two-family residence, plan design no. 80, which also was designed to resemble a single-family residence. This colonial revival plan, which featured a symmetrical façade and large two-story columns, had a large, six-room apartment on each level, as shown in Figure 2.64. Each apartment was almost identical in size and arrangement, with a prominent front porch, two bedrooms, a living room, a dining room, a kitchen, a breakfast room, a bath, and a back porch. Wilburn mentioned the demand for "two-family houses" in her description of this design, stating:

Having had considerable demand for effective two-family houses, I am here showing one that would be a credit to the highest class residential section. Such a house makes a splendid investment. For a traveling man it makes an ideal arrangement as it affords his family protection while he is away. There are individual front and rear porches and both front and rear stairways are private. The room arrangement is ideal. The basement calls for a steam heating plant, laundry tubs, and servants' toilet. The brick veneered exterior walls are relieved by the white trim and colonial columns.[59]

A two-story duplex design that has been documented in both brick and wood frame construction, plan design no. 108, shown in Figure 2.65, was published in Wilburn's second plan book. It offered a two-level apartment design, with two bedrooms and a bath, a kitchen, breakfast, and living area, as well as a large front porch on each level. In describing this two-family design, Wilburn wrote: "For the traveling man a duplex solves

FIGURE 2.63. This two-family residence was offered as a mail-order house plan in Wilburn's first plan book, *Southern Homes and Bungalows*. The floor plan showed fold-down beds in the living spaces.

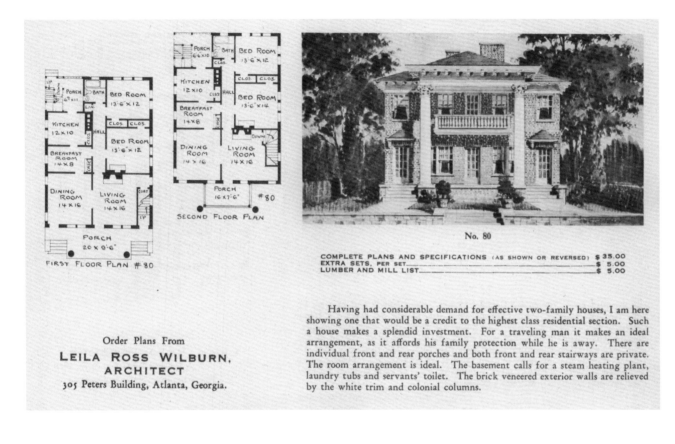

FIRST FLOOR PLAN #80

SECOND FLOOR PLAN #80

No. 80

COMPLETE PLANS AND SPECIFICATIONS (AS SHOWN OR REVERSED) $35.00
EXTRA SETS, PER SET_____$ 5.00
LUMBER AND MILL LIST_____$ 5.00

Order Plans From
LEILA ROSS WILBURN,
ARCHITECT
305 Peters Building, Atlanta, Georgia.

Having had considerable demand for effective two-family houses, I am here showing one that would be a credit to the highest class residential section. Such a house makes a splendid investment. For a traveling man it makes an ideal arrangement, as it affords his family protection while he is away. There are individual front and rear porches and both front and rear stairways are private. The room arrangement is ideal. The basement calls for a steam heating plant, laundry tubs and servants' toilet. The brick veneered exterior walls are relieved by the white trim and colonial columns.

FIGURE 2.64. Plan design no. 80 was a colonial revival–style, two-family residence designed to resemble a single-family residence. It was published in *Homes in Good Taste*, Wilburn's fourth plan book. With a six-room apartment on each level, it was one of the largest designs for a two-family residence offered in Wilburn's early plan books.

the housing problem. The large breakfast room will be found a satisfactory substitute for the dining room. The plan was drawn according to the directions of a contractor who is noted for his ability at designing 'good sellers.' It can be built on a narrow and shallow lot. I have a similar front with five regular rooms to each floor."[60] The two-family residence shown in Figure 2.66 was built in brick construction on College Avenue in Decatur, Georgia. The residence shown in Figure 2.67 was built as the reverse plan in wood frame construction in the Ansley Park neighborhood in Atlanta.

Wilburn's fifth plan book, *New Homes of Quality*, provided a mail-order stock duplex design, shown in Figure 2.68, which also was designed to look like a single family residence. The description for plan design no. 2551 read as follows:

This house was designed to be used by a mother and her married daughter. Neither family needed but one bedroom for regular use, but each had an occasional visitor. The middle bedroom therefore had a door into each hall and the guest room is used for either apartment as needed. Each apartment has its own basement and private steam heating plant. The stair

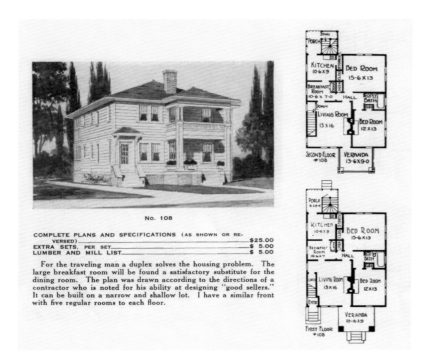

No. 108

COMPLETE PLANS AND SPECIFICATIONS (AS SHOWN OR RE-
VERSED)_____$25.00
EXTRA SETS, PER SET_____$ 5.00
LUMBER AND MILL LIST_____$ 5.00

For the traveling man a duplex solves the housing problem. The large breakfast room will be found a satisfactory substitute for the dining room. The plan was drawn according to the directions of a contractor who is noted for his ability at designing "good sellers." It can be built on a narrow and shallow lot. I have a similar front with five regular rooms to each floor.

FIGURE 2.65. One of the most popular plan book designs for a two-family residence was plan design no. 108 in *Brick and Colonial Homes*. It offered a compact floor plan with a living room, kitchen, breakfast room, and two bedrooms on each level, as well as a front porch that provided an outdoor living area for each apartment.

FIGURE 2.66. This two-family residence was built with a brick exterior on College Avenue in Decatur, Ga., from plan design no. 108. This duplex offered comfortable living spaces on each level in an attractive two-story design.

FIGURE 2.67. This two-family residence was built on 17th Street in the Ansley Park neighborhood in Atlanta as a reverse plan of design no. 108. The entrance to the first-level apartment is from the front porch; the exterior front door to the right of the porch leads to an enclosed staircase to the second-level apartment.

to the attic space is used by both families. The baths are placed close to the bedrooms and being next to the kitchen reduces the plumbing bill.

The exterior of this duplex has the appearance of a one-family house. The entrance gable is a pinkish tan stone and tones in with the red brick walls, cream trim and blended red asphalt shingle roof, a pleasing color combination being thus obtained. The gables are placed so that the front is most attractive.[61]

As Wilburn explained, this single-story duplex was designed as a two-family residence with a bilateral plan. It included identical one-bedroom apartments that were separated in the middle of the plan by stairs to the attic and basement levels. A door from each apartment to a rear bedroom provided a guest room that could be shared by both apartments.

In her description of another two-family residence offered in *New Homes of Quality*, plan design no. 2369 (see Fig. 2.69), Wilburn noted the demand for duplexes designed to look like single-family dwellings in a residential neighborhood:

Many people desire a two-family house, yet want to build in a strictly residential section. This duplex will grace any street. One family enters from the attractive arched entrance while access to the other side is thru the front porch. The house is designed so that either family may use the middle bedroom. The house was originally planned for a couple whose parents wished to live in the same house, yet leave each family perfect privacy. They intended the middle bedroom as a guest room to be used by either family. Each apartment has its own hot air furnace in the basement.[62]

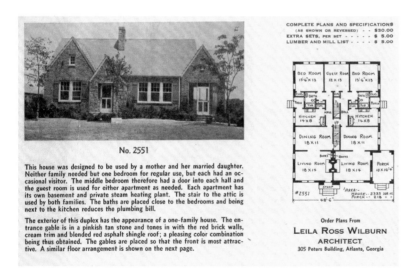

FIGURE 2.68. Plan design no. 2551 was a one-story, two-family residence designed for "a mother and her married daughter." Wilburn included it in *New Homes of Quality*, her fifth plan book. She designed the exterior to resemble a single-family residence. The shared guest room was one of the attractive features of this compact duplex design.

FIGURE 2.69. Another two-family residence designed to resemble a single-family home, plan design no. 2369 had a floor plan that was very similar to the design for plan design no. 2551, shown in Fig. 2.68. It also was offered in *New Homes of Quality*. This duplex design featured a porch for each apartment as well as a shared guest room.

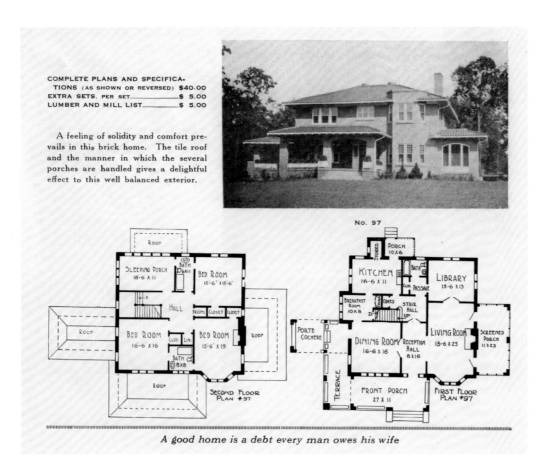

FIGURE 2.70. Plan design no. 97 in *Brick and Colonial Homes* was one of Wilburn's largest mail-order house plans. Its spacious interiors included many of the attractive features in other plan book designs, such as a large library with an adjacent bath on the first level that could function as a downstairs bedroom. A screened porch was connected to the large living room on the first level, and large corner bedrooms, baths, and a sleeping porch were located on the second level.

Presumably because of the demand for a range of housing options, Wilburn offered duplex or two-family house designs in most of her plan books. As these examples have shown, many two-family dwellings were designed to look like single-family residences, either with an apartment on each level of a two-story house or as a bilateral plan in a single story residence. While these multi-family dwellings were offered as mail-order stock plans, Wilburn's contributions also included designs for a number of large custom-designed apartment buildings, including two that are historic landmarks in Atlanta, the Rosslyn on Ponce de Leon Avenue, and Piedmont Park Apartments on 11th Avenue.[63]

A final example of a southern home built from one of Wilburn's early plan books is located in the Druid Hills neighborhood in Atlanta. As shown in Figure 2.70, plan design no. 97 was one of the largest plan designs and represents a particularly well-designed home with features that Wilburn's early plan book houses would become known for: spacious interiors, flexible living areas, quality materials, and a beautiful exterior. A

FIGURE 2.71. This two-story southern home was built on a large lot on Springdale Road in the Druid Hills neighborhood of Atlanta from plan design no. 97. Its wide roof overhangs and projecting clay tile roofs above the porte cochere and porches provide a horizontality that appears to anchor this majestic home to its beautiful site.

large front porch and open terrace across the front of the house was connected to a porte cochere on the left side, offering outdoor living spaces and the convenience of a covered connection to the vehicular drive for departures and arrivals. The brick exterior, tile roof, bay windows, and asymmetrical façade offered a mix of architectural materials and details that provided scale, balance, and charm in a uniquely American style, as shown in Figure 2.71. On the first level, a large living room to the right of the reception hall was connected to a large screen porch on the side of the house with French doors connecting the living room to the library in the rear of the house. The full bath and closet next to the library provided flexibility in converting the space to another function such as a downstairs bedroom, as Wilburn often suggested. The large kitchen, breakfast room, and dining room were designed for efficiency and practicality, with a large pantry, built in china cabinet, and back porch service area. The upstairs featured three large corner bedroooms with two baths and a large sleeping porch, like so many of Wilburn's two-story southern homes. There were closets for clothes, linens, and cleaning supplies. The large double-height bay window on the front of the house gave it a strong presence and provided extra daylight and views from the living room and front bedroom. Wilburn wrote: "A feeling of solidity and comfort prevails in this brick home. The tile roof and the manner in which the several porches are handled gives a delightful effect to this well balanced exterior."[64] As part of its unique history, for more than half a century, this house was home to several generations of the same family. Through the years it has provided comfort and elegance, offering convenience, flexibility, and accommodation, with few changes made to the original design.

As shown in this chapter, the craftsman bungalow, the post-Victorian southern home, colonial revival, and eclectic period houses based on European-inspired historical designs were the predominant house styles in Wilburn's first five plan books. These books include more than three hundred house designs and represent the most prolific period in Wilburn's architectural career. True to her ambition to supply house plans for southern homeowners and builders, in each plan book Wilburn offered a diverse range of architectural styles and floor plans that reflected the evolution of the American home. As a talented architect, a southern woman, and an advocate for homeowners, Wilburn claimed the domestic domain as her own, designing houses, publishing plan books, and creating an enduring architectural legacy of twentieth-century southern homes that are enjoyed today as twenty-first century historic homes.

CHAPTER 3

From 1930s Small to 1950s Ranch *Leila Ross Wilburn's Later Plan Book Houses*

WILBURN'S FIRST FIVE PLAN BOOKS, discussed in chapter 2, provided plan designs in architectural styles that were popular during the first three decades of the twentieth century. Houses were built from these designs throughout the Southeast during a historical period defined by economic growth, urban expansion, suburban development, and an increased demand for smaller and more modern homes.

After the publication of *New Homes of Quality* (Wilburn's fifth plan book), which offered a variety of period house designs, Wilburn's later plan books reflected a shift to much smaller house designs and simpler plans, in predominantly low-scale, one-story house designs.[1] These four plan books, published from the mid-1930s to 1960, constituted Wilburn's response to the housing needs of southern homeowners during a challenging period marked by, first, economic decline and wartime hardships, then by a post-war housing shortage and a suburban housing boom.

Most of the plan designs in these later plan books were based on two new house types, the "minimal traditional house" and the ranch house. The minimal traditional house, also referred to as the "American small home," was the small house type that emerged in response to the need for affordable houses during the dramatic economic decline of the 1930s.[2] After World War II, when a new house type, the ranch house, became the ideal suburban home of the 1950s, Wilburn offered a wide range of ranch house designs for the "average American family."[3] The new house types, both the minimal traditional house and the ranch house, offered smaller house designs that were more affordable for many Americans for whom homeownership had become almost out of reach.

This chapter will provide a general summary of Wilburn's last four plan books. Less is known about this later period in Wilburn's career, and fewer houses have been identified from her later plan books.[4] However, in offering examples from these plan books and examining some identified houses, this chapter will describe some significant changes in the American home, as well as Wilburn's contributions as a plan book architect during this historical period.

The economic downturn known as the Great Depression, which began with the stock market crash of 1929, caused high unemployment, business failures, and a tremendous loss of financial capital. The impact of the Great Depression on the housing industry throughout the United States was particularly devastating. As Gwendolyn Wright wrote in *Building the Dream: A Social History of Housing in America*, "By 1933, at the peak of the depression, there were one thousand foreclosures per week. Residential construction had plummeted to 93,000 units, down from 937,000 in 1925, and most of these were houses or apartments for the well-to-do."[5]

The federal government acted to address this crisis, most importantly by passing the Federal Housing Act of 1934—a timely piece of legislation that supported the housing industry. As Wright explained, "After the inauguration of Franklin Roosevelt, the New Deal government began a major effort to rebuild the construction industry. The landmark National Housing Act of 1934, in addition to establishing a public-housing program, set up the Federal Housing Administration (FHA) to stimulate the moderate-cost private-housing market."[6] Although specific requirements had to be met, the availability of long-term, FHA mortgages (with low down payments) and construction loans was instrumental in supporting homeownership and reviving the housing industry throughout the country.

Even with federal government programs providing assistance in financing, however, the national economic crisis demanded a radically different response on the part of residential architects and builders. To keep homeownership affordable for the middle class, smaller houses were called for—houses that were even simpler and more compact than the small house designs of previous decades. Eclectic period houses continued to be popular through the 1930s, but the widespread demand for much smaller,

affordable houses created a market for a new house type that would remain prevalent into the 1950s.[7]

In 1936, the FHA published the bulletin *Principles for Planning Small Houses*, which provided builders and homeowners with guidelines for the design of small houses. With its emphasis on simplicity, efficiency, and affordability, this publication strongly influenced the development of the minimal traditional house type. This house type in most cases followed these principles and met the FHA design specifications for small houses, and individuals who proposed projects that met these specifications were more likely to secure financing (or have it expedited).

Architecturally, the new, "minimal traditional" house type was a simple, one-story house, rectangular in form, typically with a side-gabled roof and often featuring a front cross-gable wing.[8] It usually had a wood frame exterior with a simple floor plan that provided, if designed according to FHA principles, "minimum accommodation at a minimum cost."[9] As a small, low-cost, affordable home, it was the most prevalent house type during much of the 1930s and 1940s.[10]

In *A Field Guide to American Houses*, McAlester explained how this house type answered a critical need for low-cost, small houses in the depressed economic conditions of the 1930s:

The Minimal Traditional house was "the little house that could." It was the small house that could be built with FHA-insured loans in the midst of the Great Depression between 1935 and 1940; the house that could be built quickly to accommodate millions of relocating World War II production-plant workers (1941–45); and the house that could be built rapidly during the late 1940s in large post–World War II developments (1946–49). These late-1940s developments were necessary to begin to fulfill the wartime GI Bill promise that every returning serviceman would be able to purchase a home.[11]

Just as the bungalow had represented simplicity, efficiency, and economy at the turn of the century, the minimal traditional house became the affordable small house type of the 1930s and 1940s. This house type offered a practical solution to the acute need for millions of low-cost homes. As McAlester explained, the minimal traditional house could address a diverse range of housing needs, from small, affordable homes for the middle class to temporary wartime housing and suburban homes for World War II veterans.

Small Low-Cost Homes for the South, Wilburn's sixth plan book, published in the mid-1930s, represented a new direction for Wilburn as a plan book architect.[12] In response to the need for small, affordable southern homes for 1930s suburbs, *Small Low-Cost Homes for the South* offered, as Wilburn explained, "62 designs for homes much smaller than those shown in my previous plan books."[13] Most of Wilburn's previous plan book designs had emphasized efficiency, economy, and convenience. While Wilburn's design principles remained the same, the plan designs for the minimal traditional house type in this plan book had significantly smaller rooms and simpler floor plans, some with less than a thousand square feet in a two-bedroom, one-story design, and most plan designs with less than two thousand square feet.

Many plan designs in *Small Low-Cost Homes for the South* were in the colonial revival style, which was a good economical choice given its compatibility with wood-frame construction and its enduring aesthetic appeal. The Cape Cod house, although native to New England, was a vernacular colonial revival style that was popular throughout the country. With a side gable roof form, it was a simple historical style that was often used in minimal traditional or small house designs.[14]

Although Wilburn's plan designs for small, low-cost homes were traditional in form, compact in plan arrangement, and simpler in materials, features, and finishes, they were not "minimal" in design. As Wilburn wrote in promoting her small house designs, "You can build a small house that is architecturally as correct as a larger one."[15] Even on the smallest homes, Wilburn designed porches as outdoor rooms, much like the plan designs for her larger southern homes in earlier plan books. The porches

FIGURE 3.1. The front cover of *Small Low-Cost Homes for the South*, Wilburn's sixth plan book, featured a rendering of a typical small house design. This plan book, offered in a 6-by-8-inch format, included sixty-three designs for small homes. The designs were primarily of one-story, wood-frame houses with compact floor plans that were smaller than most houses featured in Wilburn's previous plan books.

typically were on the side of the house and were connected to the small but functional living rooms. A steeply pitched roof and a permanent stair to attic storage space—common features in many of Wilburn's small house plan designs—provided space for future expansion. Wilburn's small house designs also had simple, economical architectural elements that added style, charm, and individuality to the exterior design, such as window shutters, flower boxes, porch trellises, and railings.

Interestingly, the FHA's *Principles of Planning Small Houses*, which promoted basic, low-cost, minimal traditional houses, acknowledged the importance of simple, decorative details and a pleasing exterior design that provided scale and character. It stated: "No dwelling can make a satisfactory home which provides merely for the mechanics of living. In any house, no matter how small, there must exist a sense of comfort in appointments, and a feeling of charm in its appearance and setting. . . . While it may be necessary to reduce the basic house to a box, it must nevertheless be a well proportioned box with its materials and openings treated with imagination and skill."[16] Wilburn's later plan books offered plan designs for small, low-cost homes that were both functional and beautiful. They were outstanding examples of small houses that achieved what the FHA intended in the design of affordable homes. Understanding the unique challenges of designing a small home, the FHA articulated principles intended to define the characteristics of a low-cost house, while

allowing for some freedom in the overall design: "The planning of the small house thus becomes a special art, rigidly limited by the necessity for low-cost, yet none the less exacting in its requirement for functional arrangement and esthetic satisfaction."[17] Wilburn sixth plan book offered small, well-designed houses that demonstrated her artistic abilities in designing comfortable, attractive homes that could be constructed following these guidelines and at low cost.

Figure 3.2 shows an example of a minimal traditional house in the colonial revival or Cape Cod style. This house, plan design no. 1096, was a small, two-bedroom, wood frame house with less than a thousand square feet. The living room fireplace and a gas heater in the hall between the bedrooms provided heating. The spacious living room included a dining alcove in addition to a kitchen large enough for a table and chairs. A side

FIGURE 3.2. An example of a minimal traditional house type, plan design no. 1096 was featured on the first page of *Small Low-Cost Homes for the South*. It was a small, two-bedroom home, offering an efficient design in an affordable, compact house plan.

porch was directly connected to the living room. Wilburn gave this fine example of a well-designed small home a prominent place as the first design in *Small Low-Cost Homes for the South*.

Plan designs no. 1178 and no. 1231 were two floor plan options for another small minimal traditional house in the colonial revival style, as shown in Figure 3.3. With a compact two-bedroom floor plan, each plan design was less than eleven hundred square feet. A vertical wood trellis with the diamond design at the front entrance arch and at the columns on the side porch were among the simple, attractive design features of this small home.

In addition to offering small, minimal traditional house designs, *Small Low-Cost Homes for the South* also included plans for smaller period houses, such as plan design no. 1739. As shown in Figure 3.4, Wilburn

offered a choice of two floor plans for this colonial revival–style home—one with two bedrooms and one bath, and another with three bedrooms and two baths. Along with the red brick exterior, its large living and dining rooms and screened porch were among the appealing features of this one-and-a-half-story house. Its steeply pitched roof and permanent stairs to the attic allowed for a future second-level expansion. A house built on Beech Valley Road in Atlanta using the reverse plan of this plan design is shown in Figure 3.5.[18]

Plan design no. 2065, one of the largest plan designs in *Small Low-Cost Homes for the South*, was a three-bedroom, two-bath home in the English vernacular revival style (see Fig. 3.6). The floor plan for this period house, like others that Wilburn offered in this plan book, was designed so that part of the house could be closed off and "rented as a small apartment and

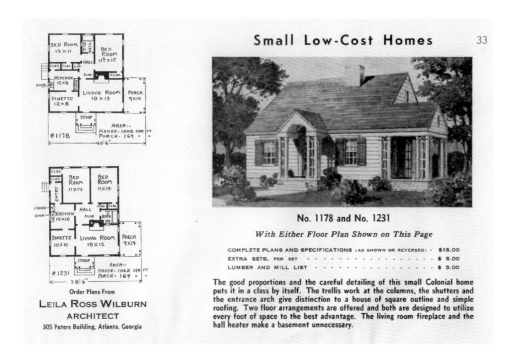

FIGURE 3.3. Wilburn provided a choice of two compact floor plans, no. 1178 and no. 1231, for this small colonial revival–style house. Each floor plan included a large living room with a fireplace that had a direct connection to a side porch on the right side of the house.

FIGURE 3.4. This colonial revival–style home was offered with a choice of five- or six-room floor plans, no. 1851 and no. 1739. Both plan designs had spacious rooms, a basement for the heating system, and an attic space large enough for two additional rooms.

FIGURE 3.5. This house was built from a reverse plan of plan design no. 1739 (shown in Fig. 3.4) on Beech Valley Road in the Morningside neighborhood of Atlanta.

Order Plans From

LEILA ROSS WILBURN

ARCHITECT

305 Peters Building, Atlanta, Georgia

Small Low-Cost Homes

41

No. 2065

The English type house here illustrated shows a pleasing combination of red brick, stone and half timber work. The herringbone brickwork in the gables adds interest to the design. The front terrace connects with living room, porch and sun room. The seven rooms are compactly arranged. By placing a temporary partition in the hall the sun room, bath room and two bed rooms on this side could be rented as a small apartment and thus help pay for the house. The living room, dining room and sun room are well connected. A steam heating plant in the basement heats the entire house. On page 24 will be found a similar floor plan with an entry entirely different outside appearance.

FIGURE 3.6. Plan design no. 2065, an English vernacular revival–style home, had a red brick exterior with timber work in a front gable with an arched entrance. It was one of the largest homes offered in *Small Low-Cost Homes for the South*, with three bedrooms, two baths, a front sunroom, a large living room with a fireplace, and a prominent front porch connected to the dining room.

thus help pay for the house."[19] Renting out part of a residence appears to have been a common strategy for homeowners, and many of Wilburn's plan book designs offered that option, as will be seen in other examples of later plan book designs. The herringbone brick in the gable ends of the porch and sunroom, the arched stone entrance, and the front terrace were among the attractive exterior features of this plan book design.

Plan design no. 1341 was a two-bedroom brick home with a prominent gabled entry, a side porch connected to the living room, and a breakfast room between the kitchen and dining areas. As shown in Figure 3.7, a permanent stair to the attic and a steeply pitched roof with dormers provided accessible attic storage space and future expansion space for the home. Wilburn called it "a pleasing design that will make an excellent home for you or a profitable investment if built to sell," suggesting that

it was an attractive plan design for a residential developer as well as a prospective homeowner.[20] Wilburn designed the house for C. E. Beem, a homebuilder who built many houses from her plan designs. Beem constructed the house shown in Figure 3.8 on Kentucky Avenue in the Virginia-Highland neighborhood in Atlanta from this plan design.[21]

Plan design no. 2569 was one of the larger houses in this plan book and was designed as a two-family residence. As Wilburn explained, "This house was designed to be used by two families until the owner needed the entire house. The first floor apartment would enter thru the porch, leaving the front entrance private for the upper floor."[22] With more than fourteen hundred square feet, the first level was a spacious two-bedroom residence and larger than several of the small homes offered in this plan book. As Wilburn explained, the second level was designed so that it could be used

COMPLETE PLANS AND SPECIFICATIONS
(AS SHOWN OR REVERSED) - - $20.00
EXTRA SETS, PER SET - - - - $ 5.00
LUMBER AND MILL LIST - - - $ 5.00

No. 1341

Here is a pleasing design that will make an excellent home for you or a profitable investment if built to sell. The proportions are good; attention is called to the arched doorway and well placed dormers. White brick walls, grey shutters and the black asphalt slate roof form a color scheme that all will approve. The convenience of the breakfast room will appeal to the housewife. The bed rooms are closely grouped around the small hall. There is attic space for storage which can be finished as an additional bed room with its private bath. The basement takes care of a hot air furnace. Living room, dining room and porch take up the front of the house.

Order Plans From

LEILA ROSS WILBURN
ARCHITECT

305 Peters Building, Atlanta, Georgia

FIGURE 3.7. Plan design no. 1341 was an attractive brick home that featured a prominent arched gable entry and a side screened porch connected to the living room. The compact two-bedroom design had a kitchen, breakfast room, and dining room, as well as a stair to the attic for future expansion.

FIGURE 3.8. This home was built from plan design no. 1341 on Kentucky Avenue in the Virginia-Highland neighborhood in Atlanta.

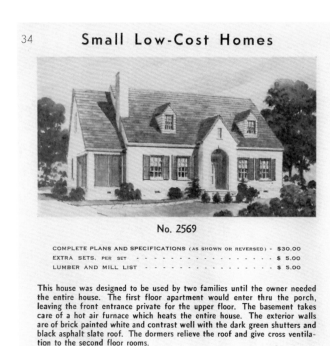

Small Low-Cost Homes

No. 2569

COMPLETE PLANS AND SPECIFICATIONS (AS SHOWN OR REVERSED) - $30.00

EXTRA SETS, PER SET · · · · · · · · · · · · · · $ 5.00

LUMBER AND MILL LIST · · · · · · · · · · · · $ 5.00

This house was designed to be used by two families until the owner needed the entire house. The first floor apartment would enter thru the porch, leaving the front entrance private for the upper floor. The basement takes care of a hot air furnace which heats the entire house. The exterior walls are of brick painted white and contrast well with the dark green shutters and black asphalt slate roof. The dormers relieve the roof and give cross ventilation to the second floor rooms.

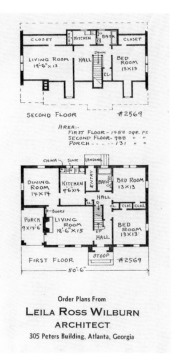

Order Plans From

LEILA ROSS WILBURN
ARCHITECT
305 Peters Building, Atlanta, Georgia

FIGURE 3.9. Plan design no. 2569, one of the duplex plan designs offered in *Small Low-Cost Homes for the South*, was a one-and-a-half-story colonial revival–style brick home. With a one-bedroom apartment on the second level and a two-bedroom apartment on the first level, it could easily be converted to a single-family residence when additional space was needed by the homeowner.

as a large one-bedroom apartment (presumably for extra income). This area could become part of the first level residence when extra space was needed. Like other two-family residences offered as plan book designs, this residential design reflected Wilburn's expertise in designing compact, two-family residences that offered affordability, flexibility, convenience, and comfort for southern homeowners (see Fig. 3.9).

Plan design no. 1856, a smaller, compact duplex design, was offered in this volume as a one-story, wood-frame minimal traditional house with colonial revival features and less than two thousand square feet (including the side porch). It offered two small one-bedroom apartments, which could share a second bedroom as a guest bedroom. Wilburn described its appeal as follows: "This duplex will be an ornament to any street and

is sure to command high grade tenants. To the casual passerby it would appear to be a private one-family house. Inside, running the depth of the structure, are two complete apartments."[23] As Wilburn explained, the plan design was a smaller version of two similar duplexes also designed to look like single-family residences that had been offered in Wilburn's fifth plan book, *New Homes of Quality*. (See Figure 2.69, plan design no. 2551, for an example of a larger duplex design with a similar floor plan.)

In a letter to Wilburn dated April 1946, a client from Cushing, Ok., requested two complete sets of reverse plans, lumber, and mill list for this plan design (no. 1856). The client enclosed a check for thirty dollars to purchase the drawings and specifications.[24] This letter, along with others that survive, indicates how the plan books functioned as catalogues for

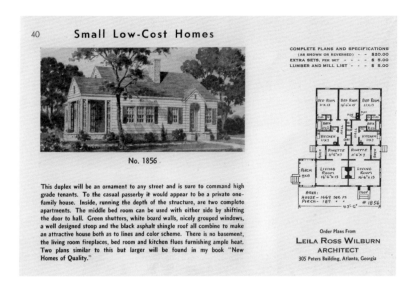

FIGURE 3.10. Another duplex designed to look like a single-family residence, plan design no. 1856 was a one-story wood-frame home with two one-bedroom apartments and a second bedroom that could be shared by both apartments.

FIGURE 3.11. The front cover of *Sixty Good New Homes*, Wilburn's seventh plan book, featured a reverse plan of design no. 2085. It was a spacious three-bedroom, two-bath home on two levels. This plan was one of Wilburn's first designs to include a one-car garage.

Wilburn's mail-order house plans. They provided homeowners and builders throughout the region with a variety of different house plans from which to choose a suitable design that could be purchased as a mail-order set of drawings for construction, regardless of location.

Wilburn's seventh plan book, *Sixty Good New Homes,* offered a range of plan designs in both brick and frame construction, with colonial revival as the predominant architectural style.[25] The estimated date of publication is the late 1930s.[26] The plans are compact designs for houses that were typically larger than those in Wilburn's previous plan book, *Small Low-Cost Homes for the South*, with houses ranging from large two-story designs and one-and-a-half-story houses to small two-bedroom houses. As with many of her previous plan designs, Wilburn often included side

porches connected to the living room as well as permanent stairs to an attic space for storage and future expansion. Several plan designs also had an attached one-car garage on the front of the house. The home shown in Figure 3.12, plan design no. 1243, is a good example of a small two-bedroom plan design from this plan book. An attractive wood and brick exterior, trellis work on the side porch, and the prominent fireplace on the front wall add charm and character to this small plan book house. A typical Wilburn design for a small house, it included an eat-in kitchen, a dining alcove, a large living room, and spacious bedrooms, with a basement area for the heating system and a permanent stairs to an unfinished attic space. It offered efficiency, comfort, affordability, and convenience as an attractive colonial revival–style home.

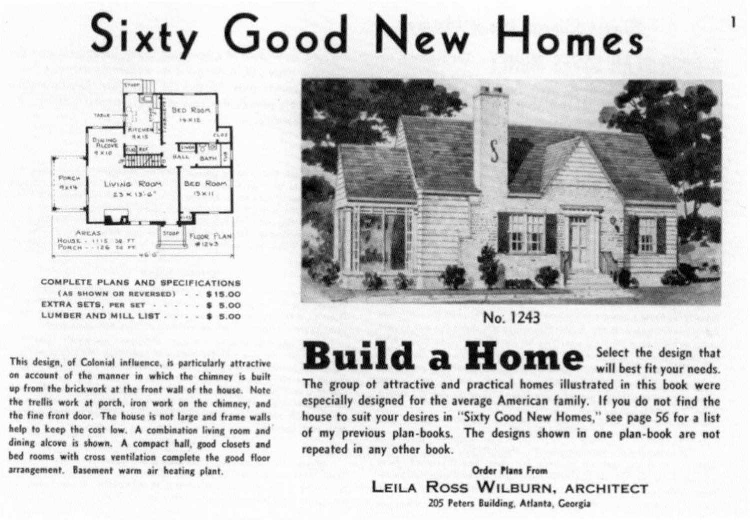

Sixty Good New Homes

1

AREAS
HOUSE - 1115 SQ FT
PORCH - 126 SQ FT

FLOOR PLAN #1243

COMPLETE PLANS AND SPECIFICATIONS (AS SHOWN OR REVERSED) - - $15.00
EXTRA SETS, PER SET - - - - - $ 5.00
LUMBER AND MILL LIST - - - - $ 5.00

This design, of Colonial influence, is particularly attractive on account of the manner in which the chimney is built up from the brickwork at the front wall of the house. Note the trellis work at porch, iron work on the chimney, and the fine front door. The house is not large and frame walls help to keep the cost low. A combination living room and dining alcove is shown. A compact hall, good closets and bed rooms with cross ventilation complete the good floor arrangement. Basement warm air heating plant.

No. 1243

Build a Home Select the design that will best fit your needs. The group of attractive and practical homes illustrated in this book were especially designed for the average American family. If you do not find the house to suit your desires in "Sixty Good New Homes," see page 56 for a list of my previous plan-books. The designs shown in one plan-book are not repeated in any other book.

Order Plans From
LEILA ROSS WILBURN, ARCHITECT
205 Peters Building, Atlanta, Georgia

FIGURE 3.12. Plan design no. 1243, a minimal traditional house in brick and wood, included two bedrooms, a large living room with a fireplace, an adjacent dining alcove, and an eat-in kitchen.

Plan design no. 1534, as shown in Figure 3.13, was a small, one-story colonial revival home that featured an attached one-car garage and a rear porch facing the backyard. Residential designs with attached garages (and later carports) began to emerge as early as the 1930s.[27] These designs contrasted earlier designs in which the garage was detached and at the rear of the property. Most middle-class households owned at least one car by the 1940s, and designers began attaching garages or carports to homes as an extension of the house plan, instead of as a separate structure located in the rear of the property. Larger lot sizes in new suburban developments offered private backyard spaces for outdoor activities and landscaped garden spaces. The primary outdoor gathering space shifted during this time from the front porch to a back porch and patio areas, which offered more privacy and a safer, quieter area away from street traffic.[28] According to Wilburn, "Sometimes it is advantageous to have the garage within the body of the house, entrance being from the front. If the rear garden is landscaped to one's liking, the placing of the living porch to get this view is desirable. This house was planned with these two ideas in mind."[29] The plan design also included a permanent staircase to an unfinished attic space, as well as a basement for the heating system, a laundry, and a toilet.

Figure 3.14 shows a house that was built from this plan design on Wieuca Terrace, in the North Buckhead neighborhood in Atlanta, by J. O. Anderson, a contractor who constructed many houses from Wilburn's house designs in this part of the city.[30] This house has undergone some renovations and changes, including the conversion of the garage to an enclosed space.

A small two-story colonial revival home with a compact design, plan design no. 1666 offered a large kitchen, lavatory, dining room, and living room on the first level and three bedrooms and a bath on the second level (see Fig. 3.15). Built-in bookshelves on either side of the fireplace, a porch connected to the living room, and a basement area were among its attractive features. The exterior façade was clad with a brick veneer on the first level and wood shingles on the second level. Trellis work on the porch and shutters added simple details to this economical design. Wilburn's description of this plan reads as follows: "This two-story Colonial home is quite inexpensive to build yet it has everything necessary to make it attractive and convenient. The fluted pilasters at the entrance, overhang at the second floor level, and trellis work at porch columns add to the character of the house."[31] The house's final selling point was its compact plan: "Note that the combined area of both floor and porch is less than 1700 square feet."[32] A house was built by contractor J. O. Anderson on Wieuca Terrace from a reverse plan of plan design no. 1666. The house has been renovated to enclose the first-level porch

No. 1534

Sometimes it is advantageous to have the garage within the body of the house, entrance being from the front. If the rear garden is landscaped to one's liking, the placing of the living porch to get this view is desirable. This house was planned with these two ideas in mind. The exterior was made attractive by the stonework, shutters and well placed dormers. The entry with its coat closet is a convenient arrangement. The end wall of the living room is made attractive by open book shelves at each side of the Colonial mantel. The breakfast room is separated from the "U" shape kitchen by a serving bar. Both bedrooms have cross ventilation and space for twin beds. The basement takes care of the hot air heating plant, laundry and servant's toilet.

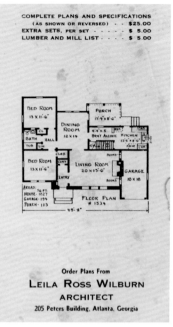

FIGURE 3.13. Plan design no. 1534 was one of Wilburn's first designs with the living porch located behind the kitchen in the rear of the house, overlooking the backyard and with an attached one-car garage. The bedrooms were designed to accommodate twin beds, and the large living room had a fireplace with built-in bookcases.

FIGURE 3.14. This house on Wieuca Terrace in Atlanta was built from plan design no. 1534.

FIGURE 3.15. Plan design no. 1666 was a small, two-story house with large living, dining, kitchen, and powder rooms on the first level and three bedrooms and a bath on the second level. A side porch was connected to the living room, and the kitchen accommodated a table and chairs.

FIGURE 3.16. This house was built on Wieuca Terrace from a reverse plan of plan design no. 1666. The side porch has been enclosed as a living space with a second-level addition.

and to build an addition on the second level above the porch, as shown in Figure 3.16.

Another example of a compact design for a three-bedroom, colonial revival style–home, plan design no. 1774, had an attractive exterior of brick with asbestos shingles, a bay window on the front of the house, and arched trellis work on the screened porch, as shown in Figure 3.17. Wilburn's description highlighted the plan's main features: "This house, of Colonial atmosphere, suggests comfortable living and has an attractiveness which is real because it is based upon sound construction and good taste. The house is of frame construction with a combination of brick veneer and asbestos shingles for exterior walls. The arch treatment of the trellis work at the porch adds a light touch. The living room is

large and well proportioned with a wide bay window, a feature that adds considerable interest to the exterior design."[33] Additional design features that enhanced this small, one-story house included spacious bedrooms, a large living room with a direct connection to the screened porch, a basement for the heating system, and a permanent stair to the attic. A house on Greenview Avenue in the Peachtree Park neighborhood in Atlanta was built by J. O. Anderson from this plan design, as shown in Figure 3.18.

In 1942 Wilburn left her architectural practice and enlisted in the Civilian Service for three years, serving in Tampa, Fla., and Washington, D.C., until October 1945.[34] When Wilburn returned home, she reopened her office in the Peters Building in downtown Atlanta, where her office had been located since 1908. The effect that this absence and the post-war

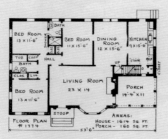

COMPLETE PLANS AND SPECIFICATIONS
(AS SHOWN OR REVERSED) - - $30.00
EXTRA SETS, PER SET · · · · · $ 5.00
LUMBER AND MILL LIST · · · · $ 5.00

Order Plans From
LEILA ROSS WILBURN
ARCHITECT
205 Peters Building, Atlanta, Georgia

No. 1774

This house, of Colonial atmosphere, suggests comfortable living and has an attractiveness which is real because it is based upon sound construction and good taste. The house is of frame construction with a combination of brick veneer and asbestos shingles for exterior walls. The arch treatment of the trellis work at the porch adds a light touch. The living room is large and well proportioned with a wide bay window, a feature that adds considerable interest to the exterior design. The kitchen arrangements permit use of a breakfast table at the dining room wall. A minimum hall gives access to bedrooms and bath. The windows have been so spaced as to provide good furniture placement. In the attic there is space for one room and a bath. The house is well heated by a basement forced warm air heating plant.

FIGURE 3.17. Plan design no. 1774 was a spacious three-bedroom, two-bath home, with a large living room on the front connected to a dining room that overlooked the backyard. The arched wood trellis work on the side porch and the bay window in the living room were among its attractive features.

FIGURE 3.18. This house was built on Greenview Avenue in Atlanta from plan design no. 1774 in *Sixty Good New Homes*, Wilburn's seventh plan book.

housing boom had on Wilburn's plan book business is not well documented. However, some surviving correspondence indicates that individuals did continue to order plan designs in the late 1940s from Wilburn's earlier published plan books, including *Homes in Good Taste* (c. late 1920s), *Small Low-Cost Homes for the South* (c. mid-1930s), and *Sixty Good New Homes* (c. late 1930s/early 1940s).[35] Presumably, in resuming her Atlanta architectural practice and plan book business at the age of sixty, Wilburn continued to advertise and sell previously published plan books and mail-order house plans to homeowners and builders, in addition to creating new plan designs for her next plan book.

In addressing the post-war housing shortage and demand for affordable homes, particularly for returning veterans, Wilburn likely reconnected

FIGURE 3.19. The front cover of *Ranch and Colonial Homes*, Wilburn's eighth plan book, featured plan design no. 2247. This ranch house was designed as a three-bedroom, two-bath home with a formal entry, an eat-in kitchen, a large living room with direct connections to the dining room and side porch, and a large study with built-in bookshelves.

with previous clients, particularly contractors, developers, and other professionals in the building industry who were involved in suburban developments. Although there was now much more demand for smaller, economical house designs, Wilburn also faced competition from a greater number of professionals who recognized the opportunities in building post-war housing developments to address the national housing shortage.[36] It is not known to what extent builders relied on Wilburn's plan books in responding to the new demand for houses in the post-war era. On a national level, however, large developers, rather than homeowners or small residential contractors, began to dominate the housing industry. Supported by federal funding offered by FHA and the Veterans Administration, they were able to leverage resources to create large-scale developments. As Dolores Hayden explained in *Building Suburbia*: "Leading the post-war housing efforts were large developer-builders who could handle the government paperwork, achieve economies of scale, and undersell small builders. They totally reorganized the industry."[37]

In the late 1940s, although economic conditions had improved, millions of Americans still needed homes. The federal government continued to offer incentives for home ownership, and suburban development became a booming industry throughout the country. Residential developments on large tracts of undeveloped land offered spacious building lots for suburban lifestyles. In this changing environment, the ranch house, which had been introduced from California, soon became the predominant house type for post-war suburbs.[38]

The ranch house was an economical one-story house type distinguished by its long, horizontal profile and low-pitched roof. Other features included a front entry under the main roof structure, a large picture window on the front of the house, and hipped or gabled roofs. It was usually designed to stretch across the front of a wide suburban lot, with carports and garages for one or two automobiles and a backyard for private outdoor space and landscaped garden areas.[39]

Earlier house types, such as the bungalow, had featured an outdoor living space on the front of the house as a covered porch or veranda. In contrast, the ranch house relocated this space to the more private backyard as a porch or open patio space. In addition, the ranch house typically had an open floor plan for its main living area. A family room or den, a game room, and an eat-in kitchen were common features that reflected a new emphasis on informal living spaces and family-centered activities. As a practical and economical home for family-oriented, post-war suburbs, the ranch house became the most popular residential style during the 1950s and 1960s.[40]

The plan designs in Wilburn's eighth plan book, *Ranch and Colonial Homes*, reflected the growing popularity of the horizontal, one-story ranch house, as well as the continuing need for small, economical house designs. This plan book included sixty-three plan designs, predominantly one-story houses, with several two-story southern colonial revival plan designs and one-and-a-half-story Cape Code–style homes. Most of the one-story houses in Wilburn's eighth plan book had a long horizontal profile and the outward appearance of a ranch house. However, they resembled the minimal traditional or American small house type in plan and overall design more than the typical ranch house. For example, all but one ranch house plan design had permanent stairs to an attic space. Although the attic was designed as storage space and not expansion space, the permanent stair was an unusual feature for the ranch house type. The floor plans of Wilburn's ranch house designs in this plan book also retained the compact floor plan of the minimal traditional house and did not have the open plan that ranch houses were known for. In addition, most of Wilburn's early ranch house plan designs included stairs to lower-level, basement areas, which provided service and utility spaces also not typically found in ranch houses.

Most of the ranch house types in *Ranch and Colonial Homes* had colonial revival architectural features such as columns, pilasters, or small pediments at the entrance. Wilburn described such features as "Colonial touches" or "of Colonial extraction" in her plan designs for houses that McAlester refers to as "styled ranch house[s]" or colonial revival ranch houses.[41] Plan design no. 2145, an example of a small Wilburn ranch house plan design, included a one-car garage attached to the screened porch adjacent to the dining room. The compact floor plan, shown in Figure 3.20, included a large living room with a fireplace, a breakfast nook in the kitchen, and a third bedroom that could be used as a den. Wilburn's description read, "Quite up to date is this little white ranch type, brick-veneer house with its six well-proportioned rooms."[42] The large picture window in the living room, the recessed front entry, the hipped roof, and the one-story structure were all typical ranch house features. Although the house was small, with fewer than eighteen hundred square feet of conditioned space, it included attic storage as well as a basement level. Its floor plan more closely resembled the minimal traditional house type than an open ranch house plan.

As shown in Figure 3.21, plan design no. 1961 offered a floor plan similar to plan design no. 2145 (shown in Fig. 3.20) without the attached garage. A large bay window in the living room was a prominent feature. This plan design was typical of Wilburn's one-story plan designs. Wilburn described it as "a house that welcomes friends and lets the family live in comfort."[43] The screened side porch that connected to the dining room provided an outdoor living area, and the wide opening between the spacious living room and dining room connected these rooms on the front of the house.

A plan design with many ranch house features, plan design no. 2346 was a compact, three-bedroom, two-bath house with an eat-in kitchen and an attached carport (see Fig. 3.22). Wilburn wrote, "This house avoids the commonplace in design; in every detail it shows unusual charm."[44] The narrow front porch with wood columns and arches provided a recessed front entry. The large dining room and living room were connected by a wide, cased opening, and a rear porch overlooked the

No. 2145

Quite up to date is this little white ranch type, brick-veneer house with its six well-proportioned rooms. The screened porch gives access to the attached garage. The floor plan calls for large rooms with practically no space wasted in halls. The front vestibule has a convenient coat closet. Among the many noteworthy features are a fireplace, a sunny breakfast corner in the kitchen, ten closets and two full baths. The den is planned so it may be used as a third bedroom. Stairs lead to attic storage and basement where heating plant, laundry and maid's toilet is located.

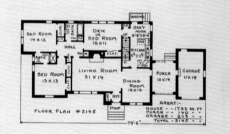

FIGURE 3.20. A compact design for a ranch house, plan design no. 2145 included a large living room with fireplace, two bedrooms, two baths, a study/bedroom, and a large kitchen with a breakfast nook facing the backyard. It had a one-car garage with a porch connection to the dining room.

No. 1961

This is a house that welcomes friends and lets the family live in comfort. The turned columns at the front stoop give a Victorian touch while the living room bay adds interest to both exterior and interior. Should the study be needed for a bedroom then the living room could have book-shelves at the opening at the side of the fireplace. The breakfast room, with its corner windows, will be used constantly. A short hall from the entry leads to the two corner bedrooms and baths. The basement has ample storage space, laundry, toilet and a forced warm air heating plant.

FIGURE 3.21. A large living room with fireplace and bay window on the front of the house and a study/bedroom overlooking the backyard were among the attractive features of plan design no. 1961. Similar to plan design no. 2145 (shown in Fig. 3.20), this small ranch house offered a very spacious three-bedroom, two-bath home in less than two thousand square feet.

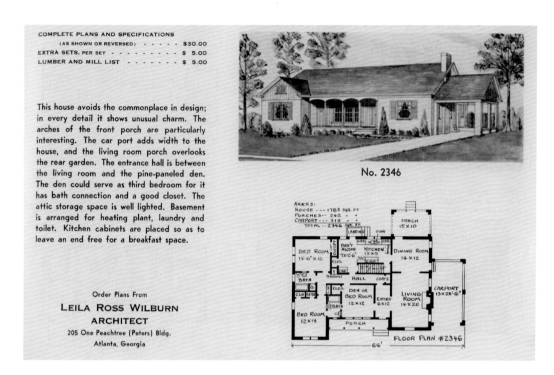

COMPLETE PLANS AND SPECIFICATIONS
(AS SHOWN OR REVERSED) - - - - $30.00
EXTRA SETS, PER SET - - - - - - - $ 5.00
LUMBER AND MILL LIST - - - - - - $ 5.00

This house avoids the commonplace in design; in every detail it shows unusual charm. The arches of the front porch are particularly interesting. The car port adds width to the house, and the living room porch overlooks the rear garden. The entrance hall is between the living room and the pine-paneled den. The den could serve as third bedroom for it has bath connection and a good closet. The attic storage space is well lighted. Basement is arranged for heating plant, laundry and toilet. Kitchen cabinets are placed so as to leave an end free for a breakfast space.

Order Plans From
LEILA ROSS WILBURN
ARCHITECT
205 One Peachtree (Peters) Bldg.
Atlanta, Georgia

No. 2346

FLOOR PLAN #2346

FIGURE 3.22. Plan design no. 2346 was another three-bedroom, two-bath house with a large living room open to the dining room. It also had a porch facing the backyard, as with many of the plans included in *Ranch and Colonial Homes*. This minimal traditional house in the ranch style offered a spacious but compact floor plan, with the heating system and laundry in the basement and an attic storage space.

backyard. The house had a stair to the basement level as well as a stair to the attic storage area.

In plan design no. 2062, a colonial revival–style ranch house, the main living spaces, including the porch, are found on the rear of the house. Wilburn explained this general design shift as follows: "This well-balanced, brick-veneered home offers a Colonial design that is sure to be popular. The front stoop will give good protection from the weather. Considerable time is usually spent in meal preparation, therefore many prefer the front kitchen where activities in the front are easily viewed. The convenient entry leads to the rear living room, dining room and porch. Privacy is thus secured and the garden becomes a part of the living quarters."[45] This plan design is one of the few in this plan book that reflect the growing popularity of the backyard as a private, outdoor space (see Fig. 3.23)

Plan design no. 3154, one of the largest plan designs offered in *Ranch and Colonial Homes*, was a two-story southern colonial house with large living room, dining room, and kitchen, as well as a breakfast room and a downstairs bedroom wing. The second level featured four bedrooms and two baths with a floor plan that was similar to many period houses and southern homes published in earlier plan books. The large side porch was directly connected to the living room, and the basement included a game room as well as traditional service and storage spaces (see Fig. 3.24).

Plan design no. 2566, another two-story house offered in *Ranch and Colonial Homes*, was a simpler four-bedroom, two-bath design with

No. 2062

This well-balanced, brick-veneered home offers a Colonial design that is sure to be popular. The front stoop will give good protection from the weather. Considerable time is usually spent in meal preparation, therefore many prefer the front kitchen where activities in the front are easily viewed. The convenient entry leads to the rear living room, dining room and porch. Privacy is thus secured and the garden becomes a part of the living quarters. A short hall gives access to den and bedrooms. Closet and bath connection makes possible the use of den as a guest room. Each bedroom has cross ventilation, two closets and space for twinbeds. Storage space in attic. Heating plant, laundry and maid's toilet in basement.

Order Plans From
LEILA ROSS WILBURN
ARCHITECT
205 One Peachtree (Peters) Bldg.
Atlanta, Georgia

FIGURE 3.23. The gabled front stoop was one of the prominent colonial revival–style features on plan design no. 2062, a one-story ranch house. The large living room and dining room of this house faced the backyard, and the rear porch was connected to the dining room. Like many other plan book houses, it had a lot of storage spaces, including a coat closet in the entry and a broom closet in the hallway.

Order Plans From
LEILA ROSS WILBURN
ARCHITECT
205 One Peachtree (Peters) Bldg.
Atlanta, Georgia

No. 3154

The Southern Colonial here shown has an unusual arrangement of rooms. The first floor bedroom, with its outside entrance, could be used as a home office. The four second floor bedrooms, two baths and large closets will be sufficient for most families. Both the living room and the adjoining porch are extra large. The separate breakfast room will be appreciated. The outside walls are brick-veneered, painted white, and the exterior design is one of charm and dignity. The basement extends under the main body of the house; has game room, toilet, laundry, storage, and forced warm air heating plant.

FIGURE 3.24. A southern colonial–style two-story home, plan design no. 3154 featured a bedroom with a full bath and closet on the first level that could be used as a private study or a master suite. The second level had four corner bedrooms, two baths, and closets, with a floor plan similar to many of Wilburn's two-story plan book houses.

No. 2566

In this house the treatment of the first floor windows and entrance shows a decided Colonial feeling. The exterior walls are brick-veneered on the first story with wide horizontal siding above. The porch off the dining room is balanced by the living room wing. Book shelves flank the living room chimney. The wide entrance hall gives space for a den at the rear. Note the coat closet and lavatory at the side of the front door. The kitchen and breakfast room are most conveniently arranged. Four corner bedrooms and two baths are shown on the second floor. In the basement you will like the game room, lavatory, laundry, and steam heating plant.

FIGURE 3.25. A two-story colonial home with a compact floor plan, plan design no. 2566 had a den overlooking the backyard, in addition to a large living room with fireplace, a formal dining room connected to a side porch, and a small breakfast room adjacent to the kitchen. The basement level provided a game room and a laundry and service area.

colonial revival features. The powder room, coat closet, and open staircase in the entrance hall are notable features (see Fig. 3.25). The den in the rear of the house connected to the breakfast room provided a family room overlooking the backyard.

Plan design no. 2268 featured a ranch house in red brick (see Fig. 3.26). Wilburn's description of this plan design read, "The clean exterior lines, wide eaves and wrought iron grills at the front stoop give this house a smart appearance. . . . The open plan of entry, living room, and dining room is to be noted. These rooms provide ample spaces for entertaining; the den for seclusion."[46] A house that was built based on plan design no. 2268 is located on Sunset Terrace in Forsyth, Georgia, and shown in Figure 3.27.[47] The changes from the plan design include windows on the front elevation and a side porch added on the right side of the house.

As shown in these examples, the designs in *Ranch and Colonial Homes* reflected a number of significant changes in the design of the modern American home. Family rooms, U-shaped kitchens with eating areas, game rooms, carports, TV rooms, backyard patios, and rear porches overlooking landscaped yards were among the new features that characterized the post-war suburban home in this plan book. They also were typical features in the plan designs offered in *Bran-New Homes*, Wilburn's ninth and final plan book, which was published in 1960.[48] *Bran-New Homes* offered plan designs that more closely resembled the typical suburban ranch house, as well as several two-story houses in the colonial revival style. Most of these plan designs were larger, three- and four-bedroom houses, including split-level designs, styled ranch houses, and two-story houses in the colonial revival style.

No. 2268

COMPLETE PLANS AND SPECIFICATIONS
(AS SHOWN OR REVERSED) - - - - - $35.00
EXTRA SETS, PER SET - - - - - - - - $ 5.00
LUMBER AND MILL LIST - - - - - - - $ 5.00

The clean exterior lines, wide eaves and wrought iron grills at the front stoop give this house a smart appearance. The exterior walls are brick-veneered with the exception of the side gables where horizontal siding is used. Here will be found something new in floor arrangement. The open plan of entry, living room and dining room is to be noted. These rooms provide ample space for entertaining; the den for seclusion. The kitchen with its bar and dining alcove is placed at the front of the house and near the front door. Easy permanent stairs lead or storage attic. The maid's toilet, laundry and heating equipment will be found in the large basement.

Order Plans From
LEILA ROSS WILBURN
ARCHITECT
205 One Peachtree (Peters) Bldg.
Atlanta, Georgia

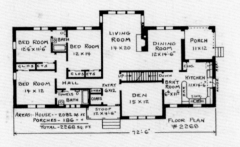

FIGURE 3.26. A three-bedroom, two-bath ranch style house, plan design no. 2268 was designed with the main living spaces—a large living room with a fireplace and a dining room—overlooking the backyard. The dining room was open to the living room with a direct connection to the porch. The den, kitchen, and breakfast room faced the front of the house. With a permanent stair to a service area in the large basement and a stair to attic storage, this house was one of the larger house designs offered in this plan book.

FIGURE 3.27. This house was built on Sunset Terrace in Forsyth, Ga., based on plan design no. 2268.

FIGURE 3.28. *Bran-New Homes*, Wilburn's ninth and last plan book, was a large-format, twenty-eight-page book with sixty-four designs. The front cover featured a rendering of plan design no. 1930, a three-bedroom, two-bath colonial revival–style ranch house.

In her eighth plan book, *Ranch and Colonial Homes*, Wilburn had offered primarily one-story ranch and colonial-style homes, but she had also introduced one split-level house design as a "brand-new type of home construction."[49] In *Bran-New Homes*, Wilburn addressed the increased popularity of this new multi-level house form, which was based on the suburban ranch house design. The growing popularity of split-level houses as a practical plan arrangement for larger ranch houses reflected the greater economy that they afforded, with the floor plan stacked vertically in three half-levels. The three levels allowed a large home to be built on a narrower lot (rather than spreading the plan out horizontally in a typical ranch house one-story plan). The split level also allowed residential spaces to be zoned according to household activity, with main living spaces on the front entrance level, private bedroom spaces on an upper level, and utility and activity rooms (and sometimes a garage) on the lower level.[50] Most plan designs in *Bran-New Homes* also featured rooms that had become popular in suburban ranch house designs, including game rooms, family rooms or dens, U-shaped kitchens with breakfast alcoves, powder rooms, and laundry/utility spaces.

Two plan designs for ranch houses, no. 3082 and no. 2162, offered similar floor plans for ranch houses that each had a more typical ranch house layout and structure than those published in the previous plan book. As a four-bedroom, three-bath home with an attached two-car garage, plan design no. 3082 had a long, horizontal profile stretched over ninety feet across the front of the lot (see Fig. 3.29). Wilburn's description read as follows: "Here is a house of quiet dignity with Colonial details at porch arches. The side entrance to the garage allows front windows and the appearance of an added room. The eight rooms and three baths are well placed. Chimney is located so as to have fireplaces in two rooms. No basement, all rooms are on the one floor."[51] Designed for the suburbs, it included a large living room with sliding glass doors that led to an outdoor backyard patio. The spacious U-shaped kitchen was open to the breakfast alcove, and the living room, dining room, and foyer were connected by large cased openings.

The smaller ranch house featured on the same page, plan design no. 2162, had a similar floor plan with smaller rooms and a carport instead of an enclosed garage (see Fig. 3.29). The family room overlooking the backyard had a fireplace and a direct connection to the outdoor patio. The exterior had many ranch house features, including a horizontal band of stone with wood siding at the front wall of the bedrooms, a planter at the recessed front entrance stoop, brick veneer siding, and a large expanse of windows in the living room.

Plan design no. 3288, another colonial ranch house, was a large, four-bedroom home with a symmetrical façade and a narrow cross gable porch at the front entrance (see Fig. 3.30). The living and dining rooms in the front of the house were connected by a cased opening. A large family room with fireplace had built-in bookcases and was connected by sliding doors to a backyard patio. The kitchen had a breakfast alcove and an adjacent utility room for laundry space, and the two-car garage included large storage rooms. Permanent stairs provided access to attic storage and a basement level with a game room, furnace, and toilet.

Plan designs for a small ranch house and a Cape Cod colonial house were featured together on a single page of *Bran-New Homes*, representing two popular house styles offered in this plan book (see Fig. 3.31). The smaller design—plan design no. 2431, a three-bedroom, two-bath ranch house—included a large living room with fireplace and built-in bookshelves on the front of the house with a U-shaped kitchen open to the family room. The family room had sliding doors to a large back yard patio, and the one-car garage including a large storage room for the heating system. Wilburn claimed, "Everyone will like this all-on-one-floor house with its turned columns at porch and old brick walls."[52] The Cape Cod house featured on the same page, plan design no. 2543, was a one-and-a-half-story house with a compact floor plan that included a large living

FIGURE 3.29. The second page of *Bran-New Homes* included plan design no. 3082, a colonial revival–style ranch house with attached garage, and plan design no. 2162, a ranch house with an attached carport. Both plans had a family room with sliding doors to a backyard patio.

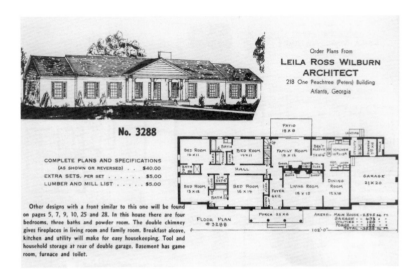

FIGURE 3.30. Plan design no. 3288 was a colonial ranch house that had a bedroom wing on the right side of the house with four bedrooms and two baths. This plan arrangement was similar to that used for the second level of many of Wilburn's two-story southern homes. With an attached garage, a family room connected to a backyard patio, and a basement with a game room and service area, this plan design was one of the largest offered in *Bran-New Homes*.

FIGURE 3.31. A three-bedroom, two-bath ranch style house, plan design no. 2431 had an attached one-car garage and a family room overlooking the backyard and connected to an outdoor patio. Plan design no. 2543 was a one-and-a-half-story, Cape Cod–style home with a compact floor plan that included a U-shaped kitchen open to the family room, which also overlooked the backyard.

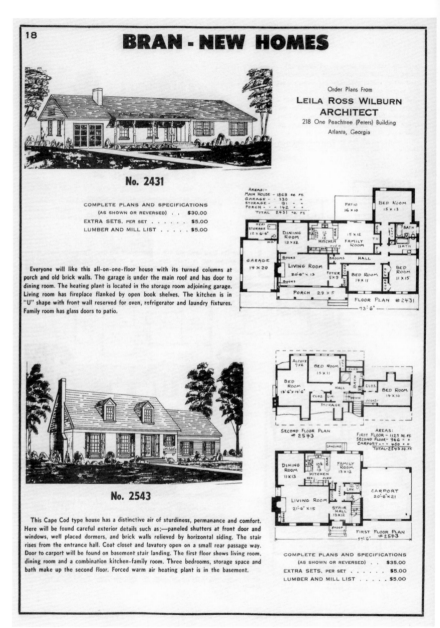

room connected to a rear dining room and a U-shaped kitchen open to a family room. Wilburn described it as follows: "This Cape Cod type house has a distinctive air of sturdiness, permanence and comfort. Here will be found careful exterior details such as;—paneled shutters at front door and windows, well placed dormers, and brick walls relieved by horizontal siding. The stair rises from the entrance hall. Coat closet and lavatory open on a small rear passage way. Door to carport will be found on basement stair landing."[53] The house had a two-car carport and a basement for the heating system. Unlike most of Wilburn's plan designs, this house had no porch space, although there was a connection from the family room to the backyard area.

One example of one of the split-level ranch houses featured in this plan book, plan design no. 3531, had a typical floor plan with the living areas on the main, entry level and four bedrooms, two baths, and closets on the upper level (see Fig. 3.32). The lower level included a large play room and bath, a shop and a utility room for laundry and appliances, and a separate room for the furnace and water heater. Wilburn's description read: "Here the strong Colonial feeling is created thru the use of many paneled windows, shutters and the gracious front porch. Note the low, inviting lines and the door from garage to kitchen. The large family room is made attractive by the brick fireplace, book shelves and glass sliding doors looking out on the rear patio. The adjoining kitchen has built-in oven, cooktop on

FIGURE 3.32. An example of a split-level ranch house, plan design no. 3531 included the living spaces and an attached one-story garage on the first floor level, with the four bedrooms and two baths a half-level above the main level. The lower level included a large shop space, an open play room, bath, and utility room.

counter and breakfast nook. The compact plan yields a large living room, dining room, family room and four bedrooms."[54] The kitchen was a large L-shape design with space for a table and chairs adjacent to the family room. The one-car garage had a large storage room with a tool room that was accessible from the backyard for garden tools and equipment.

Another typical ranch house with colonial revival features was offered with a choice of floor plans; these plans were offered as plan design no. 2360 and plan design no. 2664. The plans included an eat-in kitchen with a washer/dryer utility area near the two-car carport and a choice of three or four bedrooms (see Fig. 3.33). The living room and dining room were located on the front of the house near the entry foyer. The large family room featured a fireplace and sliding doors that connected to the backyard patio. Wilburn's description read: "Two floor plans are offered to fit the simple roof lines designed for this house. The outstanding feature is the iron trellis porch columns."[55] Contractor J. O. Anderson built a house in Wesley Walk, a suburban neighborhood in northwest Atlanta, from plan design no. 2360, as shown in Figure 3.34. The changes that have been made to the existing residence include a garage where the carport was located.

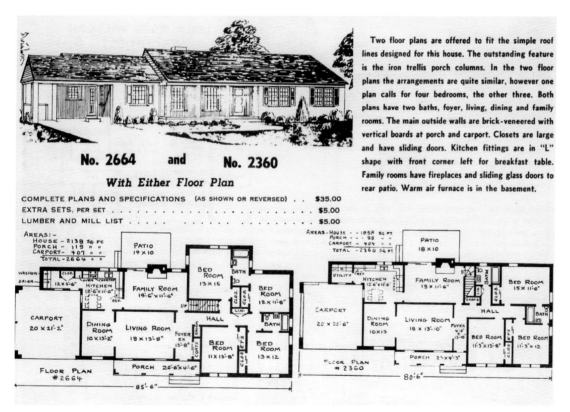

FIGURE 3.33. This ranch house was offered with a choice of two floor plans, one with four bedrooms (no. 2664) and one with three bedrooms (no. 2360). Both plans had an eat-in kitchen with adjacent utility room, a family room with sliding doors to a backyard patio, and an attached, two-car carport.

FIGURE 3.34. This house was built from plan design no. 2360 on Sequoyah Drive in the Wesley Walk neighborhood in Atlanta.

In her later plan books, Wilburn continued to offer plan designs in a wide range of architectural styles, house sizes, and modern conveniences, most of which differed substantially from those published in her earlier plan books. Most significantly, Wilburn designed many minimal traditional type houses, which represent the smallest house type of the time. As discussed, the minimal traditional house played a vital role in providing affordable, efficient homes for millions of Americans during the 1930s and 1940s. In postwar years, the horizontal, one-story ranch houses were popular as expansive designs for larger homes, reflecting changes in residential lifestyles, as well as changes in financing, developing, and constructing the suburban home.

Houses from Wilburn's later plan books, which predominantly reflected these two house types, represented not only changes in the design of the American home but also a timely response to a national need for smaller homes that more Americans could afford. Future fieldwork and research related to these later plan book designs will provide a better understanding of Wilburn's influence on suburban development and homeownership during this period. The known evidence suggests that Wilburn continued to contribute significantly to the development of housing for the middle class with her mail-order house designs offered in these later plan books.

CHAPTER 4

Learning from Wilburn in the Twenty-First Century

IT HAS BEEN more than a hundred years since Leila Ross Wilburn, a twenty-nine-year-old architect, a southern woman, and a resident of Decatur, Georgia, began her plan book business in Atlanta in 1914. As a plan book architect, Wilburn supplied economical house plans for southerners who shared a desire to own their own home. Her primary ambition—to address the need for smaller, well-designed homes for the middle class—became her life's work. For more than five decades, Wilburn's plan books offered mail-order house plans that could be purchased for a fraction of the cost of custom-designed house plans. In providing her plans in a range of architectural styles and economical designs, Wilburn became an advocate for homeowners and a champion of the middle class.

Since Wilburn's death in 1967, many individuals have made important discoveries that have expanded our knowledge of her plan book houses and of her architectural career.[1] Researchers and homeowners are among those who have provided historical information and documentation about Wilburn and about her influence as a plan book architect. The houses built from her plan designs also offer valuable insights, and further study of these plan book houses will contribute to our understanding of their enduring value and popularity as historic southern homes.[2]

This chapter examines several plan book houses that have been surveyed and documented as twenty-first century residences. It discusses the ways in which these houses have aged gracefully, adapting and changing over time to accommodate new generations of homeowners while retaining their authenticity as historic plan book houses. These particular examples were selected to represent a diverse collection of house types and styles that have many of the enduring qualities and design characteristics that Wilburn's plan book houses are known for. They include a craftsman southern home, a colonial revival home,

FIGURE 4.1. Many of the historic homes on Adams Street in Decatur, Ga., such as the one shown in this photograph, were built from plan designs that were offered in Wilburn's first two plan books.

a Mediterranean-inspired period home, a one-story Spanish revival–style home, and an English vernacular revival–style home. Most are located in the Atlanta area, with one particularly fine example of a small, Spanish revival–style home in Athens, Georgia, where many plan book houses were built. These examples of plan book houses, like so many others, reflect Wilburn's design response to her own statement as a young architect in 1921: "What we most need in America is a better class of small domestic architecture, one which shall provide us with homes more wholesome in their external appearance and more satisfying in their interior arrangement and finish."[3] As such, they represent what perhaps is Wilburn's most enduring legacy as a plan book architect.

As discussed in chapter 2, some outstanding examples of Wilburn's early plan book houses were built on Adams Street in Decatur, Georgia (see Fig. 4.1). Two southern homes on this street, one in the craftsman style, and the other in the colonial revival style, are featured in this chapter. Now part of the McDonough–Adams St.–King's Highway (MAK) Historic District, this neighborhood has changed little in scale and character since it was first developed in the early 1900s and continues to be an attractive, desirable neighborhood for Decatur residents.

A particularly fine example of a two-story southern home designed in the craftsman style on Adams Street was built from plan design no. 629, which was published in Wilburn's first plan book, *Southern Homes and Bungalows* (see Fig. 4.2). Designed when the craftsman style was particularly popular in the early twentieth century, this southern home has craftsman features such as wide overhangs, wood roof brackets, a stone foundation, wood siding on the first level, and wood shingle siding on the second level. A prominent front porch across the entire length of the house has wooden columns resting on stone pedestals with a wood railing. A photograph taken in 1993 shows the southern home built on Adams Street from this plan, with the front porch enclosed as a screened porch (see Fig. 4.3). Another photograph taken more than twenty years

later, in 2014, shows the home after the exterior was restored by the current residents (see Fig. 4.4).

Like many of Wilburn's two-story southern homes, this house is based on a typical four-square house plan. The second level had four large bedrooms, a hall with linen storage, and a bath. The spacious corner rooms on each level and windows on two exterior walls provided balanced daylight as well as fresh air and ventilation, which Wilburn considered essential for southern homes. Wilburn advised in one of her building tips in her third plan book, "Have plenty of windows, sunlight is cheaper than doctor's bills."[4] She described this eight-room, two-story home in this way:

> For a small house, this two story one has quite a large appearance. The first story walls are weatherboarded and the second shingled. The gables give quite a different effect from the plain hip roof usually used on a house of this shape.
>
> The living room is large and connects both parlor and dining room. By using the serving pantry the rear porch is reached without passing through the kitchen or dining room. No space is wasted on the second floor. Besides the grates provision is made for heating the house by furnace in the basement. The first story height is ten feet and the second nine and a half feet.[5]

One of Wilburn's first plan designs for a small, two-story house, this craftsman home was designed with a simple floor plan and attractive features that made it an efficient and comfortable home. The spacious (21-by-16-foot) living room was designed as a front corner room with large windows, a prominent fireplace, and an open staircase to the second level (see Fig. 4.5). High ceilings on both levels with large windows and corner rooms contributed to the sense of spaciousness. Its adjacent living spaces connected by wide openings on the first level allowed these rooms to be used for multiple functions, which was a popular feature in early twentieth-century homes. The "serving pantry," a wide passage from the

Design No. 629

F OR a small house this two-story one has quite a large appearance. The first story walls are weatherboarded and the second shingled. The gables give quite a different effect from the plain hip roof usually used on a house of this shape.

The living room is large and connects with both parlor and dining room. By using the serving pantry the rear porch is reached without passing through the kitchen or dining room. No space is wasted on the second floor. Besides the grates provision is made for heating the house by furnace in the basement. The first story height is ten feet and the second nine and a half feet.

FIGURE 4.2. Plan design no. 629 in *Southern Homes and Bungalows* was a craftsman-style southern home with a spacious interior and a compact floor plan. Like many of Wilburn's southern homes that were based on the four-square house type, it had four rooms on each level, a front porch that served as a functional outdoor living room, and a basement to accommodate a modern heating system.

FIGURE 4.3. This photograph (c. 1993) shows a southern home built on Adams Street in Decatur, Ga., from plan design no. 629. At that time, the front porch had been enclosed as a screened porch and an awning had been installed above the entrance.

FIGURE 4.4. This later photograph of the house on Adams Street built from plan design no. 629 was taken in 2014, after the homeowners had restored the exterior to its original design. The wide roof overhangs with wood brackets, the wooden porch columns on stone pedestals, and the use of natural materials on the exterior were among the craftsman design details on this southern home.

FIGURE 4.5. This interior photograph of the craftsman-style southern home built on Adams Street in Decatur from plan design no. 629 shows the main living area and open staircase to the second level.

FIGURE 4.6. This interior photograph of the home built from plan design no. 629 shows the renovated kitchen, with new cabinets, appliances, fixtures, and finishes in the original kitchen space.

living room to the back porch, was an unusual feature that served as a back hallway. And, like most houses of this period, a large kitchen with storage space and a back porch were located in the rear of the house. The kitchen space in this house has been renovated with new cabinets, fixtures, and appliances installed in the original kitchen space to make it more functional for the twenty-first century household, as shown in Figure 4.6. Other rooms in this southern home, including the parlor, dining room, and upstairs bedrooms, continue to be used in much the same way as they were designed, with few changes and no substantial alterations to the original design.

Another distinctive, two-story southern home that also was built on Adams Street in Decatur was offered in Wilburn's second plan book, *Brick and Colonial Homes*, as plan design no. 70 (see Fig. 4.7). It was designed as a smaller, two-story home in the colonial revival style with a front stair hall, large dining room, living room, and kitchen on the first level and four bedrooms and a bath on the second level. The porch extended across the front façade. From the front porch, the recessed entry led into the large stair hall with an open staircase to the second level. The large living room to the left of the stair hall and the dining room to the right of the stair hall both had large bay windows with window seats. The living room was designed with a fireplace and windows on three sides and was open to the stair hall and dining room across the front of the house. The abundance of daylight and views in each room is a particularly appealing feature that contributes to the sense of spaciousness and comfort in this colonial revival–style home. Wilburn wrote, "All rooms in this Colonial house are full two-story in height, but the main roof extends down over the front veranda to give a half-story effect. The front bays give added charm to the living and dining rooms."[6] This plan design also included a large kitchen with breakfast room behind the dining room, a walk-in pantry storage with a back porch and service stair access to the second level, and an enclosed stair to the basement level.

The colonial revival–style home built on Adams Street from this plan has been well-preserved and, except for a renovated kitchen area, there have been few alterations to the original plan. Figure 4.8, a photograph of the house taken in 1993, shows the main roof extending over the large front porch, which gave the house a smaller appearance. The photograph of the house shown in Figure 4.9, which was taken in 2016, provides another street view of the front of this beautiful historic home.

An attractive design for a Mediterranean-inspired period home was built on North Decatur Road in Decatur from a plan offered in *Ideal Homes of Today*, Wilburn's third plan book. Plan design no. 1008 had a floor plan that was similar to other smaller, two-story plan book houses and featured a beautiful stucco exterior with red-tile roof, windows, shutters, and French doors with iron railings, as shown in Figure 4.10. Wilburn's description of this period home read as follows:

> The use of stucco over hollow clay tile is becoming more popular every day and a particularly charming design for a small home of this material is shown here. The white walls are relieved by the red tile roof, dark shutters and iron railings. The plan is one of the most compact shown, the partitions are simple yet so arranged as to give ideal rooms on both floors. This design would also look well if built of wide white siding. A hot air furnace and two fireplaces provide heat.[7]

With 2,280 square feet and an additional 270 square feet of porch space, this plan design was another example of a smaller two-story period house with spacious interiors, beautiful craftsmanship, and a simple exterior design. It featured a large living room, approximately 15 by 26 feet, extending the entire width of the house. Windows and French doors provided light on three sides, with a fireplace centered on the side wall. A kitchen, storeroom, and back porch were located in the rear of the house. A breakfast room between the kitchen and dining room provided a convenient, informal eating area. A "living porch" was located on the side of the house

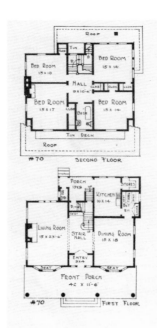

NO. 70

COMPLETE PLANS AND SPECIFICATIONS (AS SHOWN OR REVERSED) $20.00
EXTRA SETS, PER SET_____ $ 5.00
LUMBER AND MILL LIST_____ $ 5.00

All rooms in this Colonial house are full two-story in height, but the main roof extends down over the front veranda to give a half-story effect. The front bays give added charm to the living and dining rooms. The floor plan deserves to be closely studied. The plan includes fireplace and hot air heat.

FIGURE 4.7. Plan design no. 70 was a colonial revival–style home in Wilburn's second plan book, *Brick and Colonial Homes*. The large front porch, central stair hall, windows seats in the living and dining rooms, breakfast room, and large kitchen were among its attractive features.

FIGURE 4.8. This photograph, taken in 1993, shows the two-story colonial revival–style home built on Adams Street in Decatur from plan design no. 70. This street view of the house looked very similar to the photograph in FIGURE 4.7 from Wilburn's 1921 plan book.

FIGURE 4.9. This photograph of the two-story home built on Adams Street in Decatur from plan design no. 70 was taken in 2016 and shows the well-preserved exterior and prominent front porch that extends across the front of the house.

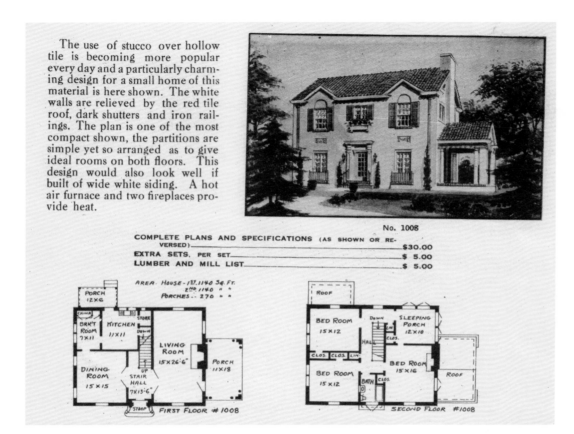

The use of stucco over hollow tile is becoming more popular every day and a particularly charming design for a small home of this material is here shown. The white walls are relieved by the red tile roof, dark shutters and iron railings. The plan is one of the most compact shown, the partitions are simple yet so arranged as to give ideal rooms on both floors. This design would also look well if built of wide white siding. A hot air furnace and two fireplaces provide heat.

No. 1008

COMPLETE PLANS AND SPECIFICATIONS (AS SHOWN OR REVERSED)_____$30.00
EXTRA SETS, PER SET_____$ 5.00
LUMBER AND MILL LIST_____$ 5.00

FIGURE 4.10. Plan design no. 1008 was an attractive Mediterranean-inspired period house offered in Wilburn's third plan book. It was designed as a small, two-story home with spacious rooms, including a central hall and open staircase and a large living room that extended the width of the house and was connected to a large side porch.

and connected to the living room. The original second-level plan had a full bath, central hall, three large corner bedrooms, and a sleeping porch, with closets for each space.

Figure 4.11 shows a house built from the reverse plan on North Decatur Road in the Druid Hills neighborhood in Atlanta. In 2015, the present owners of this historic home completed extensive renovations, including exterior restoration of stucco walls, wood shutters, front door, and iron railings, as shown in Figures 4.11 and 4.12. The original gable peaks above the second-level windows, which had been removed, were rebuilt to restore

the house to its original exterior design. The red clay tile roof had been removed and replaced with an asphalt shingle roof, which remains.

Interior renovations have included a new modern kitchen on the first level and a master suite on the second level. The side porch was enclosed as a sunroom, preserving the views and connections to the outdoors, as an informal sitting area adjacent to the living room. These interior renovations have accommodated the needs of a twenty-first-century household without significantly changing the character and charm of the original design. Most rooms, including the large living room, the dining room,

FIGURE 4.11. A home on North Decatur Road in the Druid Hills Historic District in Atlanta was built from a reverse plan of plan design no. 1008. This photograph shows the house after the exterior was restored in 2015 by the current homeowners. The side porch adjacent to the living room was enclosed and is used as an informal sitting area.

FIGURE 4.12. The street view of the home built from the reverse plan of plan design no. 1008 shows the restored stucco exterior and the simple massing of this elegant 1920s period home.

and the entrance stair hall have retained their original design and function (see Figs. 4.13 and 4.14). The iron decorative railings and French doors are among the attractive architectural features on the front of the home (see Fig. 4.15). This house is located in the Druid Hills Historic District, and it contributes to the architectural significance of this historic neighborhood as a beautiful example of a 1920s period house from Wilburn's third plan book.

FIGURE 4.13 The spacious dining room in the period home built from the reverse plan of plan design no. 1008 continues to be used as it was originally designed. The wide cased opening connects the dining room to the front stair hall shown in FIGURE 4.14.

FIGURE 4.14. The stair hall in the southern home built from the reverse plan of plan design no. 1008, shown in FIGURE 4.10, has an open staircase leading to the second level.

FIGURE 4.15. The ornamental iron railing and French doors were attractive architectural features of the dining room and the living room on the front façade of this historic home built from the reverse plan of plan design 1008. The home is located on North Decatur Road in the Druid Hills neighborhood in Atlanta.

When Wilburn's fourth plan book, *Homes in Good Taste*, was published in the late 1920s, the popularity of the bungalow was in decline, with English vernacular and European-inspired period houses becoming more popular, as discussed in chapter 2. The demand for small, one-story houses had not diminished, however, and this plan book offered many smaller, period homes in a variety of historical styles. An outstanding example from this plan book, plan design no. 1214, first discussed in chapter 2, was a charming design for a small Spanish colonial revival home. It was particularly appealing as both a small house design and as an attractive historical style. As shown in Figure 4.16, it was designed as a one-story home with a stucco exterior, clay tile eaves,

a screened porch with arched openings, an open front terrace, and a clay tile chimney top. With a total interior area of less than fifteen hundred square feet, the compact floor plan included three bedrooms, a kitchen, a breakfast room, a dining room, a large living room, and a basement with a steam heating plant. The reverse plan of this design was built in the Cobbham Historic District in Athens, Georgia, ca. 1927 (see Fig. 4.17).

The current owners undertook an exterior restoration, interior renovation, and expansion of this house as a multi-year project beginning in 2013 that included an addition designed to complement the historic house.[8] Figure 4.18 shows the house before this work was begun. The project included new stucco exterior walls, arched openings, and tile overhangs above windows (see Fig. 4.19).[9] It also included a new living room and master suite in the new addition behind the original structure, with a large, open kitchen as part of the expansion (see Fig. 4.20). The beautifully restored exterior of this historic home, with a new chimney cap rebuilt as it was originally designed, is shown in Figure 4.21.

As discussed in chapter 3, Wilburn's sixth plan book, *Small Low-Cost Homes for the South*, offered minimal traditional house designs, as well as a number of attractive, one-story period houses that were designed to be small, economical homes. Plan design no. 1991, an English-inspired period home offered in this plan book, was distinguished by its English vernacular, curved-brick entrance, which Wilburn referred to as "the Norman tower" (see Fig. 4.22). Designed as a three-bedroom, two-bath home with less than two thousand square feet, the plan was spacious but compact, offering comfort and efficiency in a one-story design. A breakfast room between the dining room on the front of the house and the kitchen in the back served as an informal eating area. A large basement had space for a heating system, laundry, and service area. A side porch connected to the living room provided a pleasant outdoor living space. Wilburn's description read as follows:

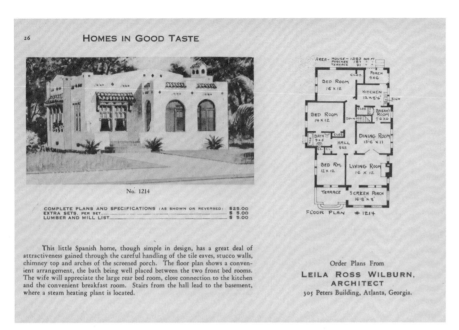

FIGURE 4.16. Wilburn's fourth plan book, *Homes in Good Taste*, featured a one-story, Spanish colonial revival–style home with a compact floor plan. Plan design no. 1214 was a charming, small house design for a three bedroom home with less than thirteen hundred square feet, as shown in the floor plan.

FIGURE 4.18. This photograph shows a side view of the exterior of the house built from the reverse plan of plan design no. 1214 on Cobb Street in Athens, Ga., before it was restored.

FIGURE 4.17. A house on Cobb Street in the Cobbham Historic District in Athens, Ga., was built from the reverse plan of plan design no. 1214 in c. 1927. The arched openings on the screened porch, tile eaves, and chimney cap were among the distinctive Spanish colonial revival features on this small 1920s period house.

FIGURE 4.19. The exterior restoration work in progress is shown in this photograph of the Cobb Street house in Athens, Ga., built from the reverse plan of plan design no. 1214.

FIGURE 4.20. A new kitchen space was part of the new construction and expansion in the rear of the Cobb Street house built from the reverse plan of plan design no. 1214.

FIGURE 4.21. The exterior restoration work for the Cobb Street house in Athens, Ga., included new stucco walls and a new chimney cap as shown in this photograph taken in 2016.

In this house the Norman tower is the outstanding feature. Of common brick walls painted grey with a touch of half-timber at the tower cornice an effect is obtained that is quite pleasing. Entrance to the living room is thru a large vestibule, a desirable feature. The porch, living room and dining room take up the entire front of the house. A cross hall gives access to all rooms. It is seldom that a plan is found with three corner bed rooms all on one floor. Each bed room has direct connection with one of the two baths. The breakfast room is large and made attractive by the corner cupboards. Sink and china cases take up the outside wall of the kitchen. The basement takes care of the laundry tray, servant's toilet and steam heating plant.[10]

A house built from this plan design in the Morningside–Lenox Park neighborhood in Atlanta was renovated in the 1960s by the current homeowners in order to expand the living spaces and to create a more contemporary interior. The renovation included a larger kitchen space, a bay window in the dining room, and an enclosed side porch on the front of the house (see Fig. 4.23). Like many of Wilburn's plan book houses, this house had a permanent stair to a large attic space, which was renovated into an open office space above the living room. The living room ceiling was removed to create a two-story living space, with a second-level office loft (open to the living room below), as shown in

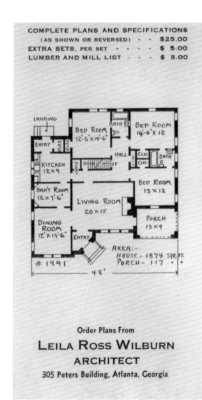

COMPLETE PLANS AND SPECIFICATIONS
(AS SHOWN OR REVERSED) - - $25.00
EXTRA SETS, PER SET - - - - $ 5.00
LUMBER AND MILL LIST - - - $ 5.00

Order Plans From
LEILA ROSS WILBURN
ARCHITECT
305 Peters Building, Atlanta, Georgia

No. 1991

In this house the Norman tower is the outstanding feature. Of common brick walls painted grey with a touch of half-timber at the tower cornice an effect is obtained that is quite pleasing. Entrance to the living room is thru a large vestibule, a desirable feature. The porch, living room and dining room take up the entire front of the house. A cross hall gives access to all rooms. It is seldom that a plan is found with three corner bed rooms all on one floor. Each bed room has direct connection with one of the two baths. The breakfast room is large and made attractive by the corner cupboards. Sink and china cases take up the outside wall of the kitchen. The basement takes care of the laundry tray, servant's toilet and steam heating plant.

FIGURE 4.22. Plan design no. 1991 was an English vernacular revival–style house with a distinctive entrance and a charming exterior. It was offered in Wilburn's sixth plan book, *Small Low-Cost Homes for the South.*

FIGURE 4.23. This house was built from plan design no. 1991 on Plymouth Road in the Morningside–Lenox Park neighborhood in Atlanta. When it was renovated in the 1960s, a bay window and an enclosed side porch on the front of the house were among the changes made to the original design.

Figures 4.24 and 4.25. A bay window was added in the dining room on the front of the house, as shown in Figure 4.26, providing more natural light. These renovations created more spacious interiors, adapting the original design to current household needs and increasing its functionality, while preserving original design features and its unique architectural style.

As shown in these examples, the design features that made Wilburn's plan book houses attractive homes in the twentieth century continue to have enduring appeal and value in the twenty-first century. Although many of these houses have undergone renovations and expansions, homeowners have taken care to preserve the historical styles and architectural features of these plan book houses. Designed for flexibility, economy, convenience, and comfort, they are Wilburn's legacy. With simplicity, character, and style, they continue to enhance the places where they are located and to enrich the lives of the people who know them. As historic homes they have earned their place in their communities. Collectively, they represent some of the finest examples of southern vernacular houses to emerge from the plan book tradition.

FIGURE 4.24. The renovation of the house built from plan design no. 1991 (shown in FIGURE 4.23) created a beautiful, two-story living room space with an open loft space above.

FIGURE 4.25. This interior photograph of the house built from plan design no. 1991 shows the view from the second level loft space, looking down into the living room below.

FIGURE 4.26. This interior photograph of the home built from plan design no. 1991 shows the dining room space with the new bay window addition, which provided more natural light and a better connection to the outdoors.

Leila Ross Wilburn's Custom Commissions and Non-Residential Work

Leila Ross Wilburn's prolific career as a plan book architect included the publication of nine plan books, hundreds of mail-order plan designs (published in her plan books), and the many homes built from her mail-order house designs throughout the South, as discussed in chapters 1 through 4. This appendix examines an aspect of Wilburn's architectural legacy that is less well known—her architectural commissions for institutional, commercial, and apartment buildings.

Identification and documentation of these custom design commissions has been challenging, since many of the records of these projects are incomplete (including their locations, design drawings, and dates of construction), and some of the buildings have been demolished. However, records do give an indication of work on many such projects, some quite large and involving significant budgets. For example, listings in the *Manufacturers Record*, a publication of the Southern Association of Science and Industry that gave public notice of all current construction projects by state, and the *Industrial Index*, published in Columbus, Georgia, announce the commission or completion of many specific buildings, with details about design and construction, primarily in the 1910s.[1] Such buildings helped respond to the rising demand for housing discussed in chapter 2, and they also, given that many were located in the Midtown neighborhood in Atlanta, may have been commissioned to fill a specific need following the destruction of property by the fire of 1917.[2] Even though some of these buildings have been demolished, other commissions from this period survive as well-known architectural landmarks.

This appendix will examine four of Wilburn's custom commissions that have been documented in detail, including two apartment buildings that have been renovated into attractive condominiums in the Midtown neighborhood in Atlanta. It will also provide information about additional commissions discovered by the authors, including some records of buildings that have not been located. This information is offered as an incomplete survey of known non-residential custom design work that Wilburn undertook during her early years of architectural practice. Wilburn's custom commissions are not as well documented as her plan book designs, and none of the original floor plans or construction drawings from these projects are known to exist. However, the four major projects introduced in this appendix give a sense of the extent of Wilburn's practice in the early years, during the time that she was determining the direction of her career.

Soon after Wilburn left the Atlanta architectural firm B. R. Padgett & Sons in 1908 to begin her own practice, she contributed to the construction of a new Young Men's Christian Association (YMCA) building for the Georgia Military Academy in College Park, Georgia, just south of Atlanta. According to a recent history of the Georgia Military Academy (now the private coeducational school Woodward Academy), the building contained a social room, a game room, a room for Bible study, and a chapel, and at the time it "was probably the only Y.M.C.A. building of its kind in any boys' school in the world."[3] The building appears to have been an initiative for which Mrs. Alonzo Richardson, a civic and church

FIGURE APP.1. Photo of the Young Men's Christian Association (YMCA) building from the 1919 Georgia Military Academy yearbook, *The Arsenal*.

include large wood brackets at the roof cornice and balconies, a wide eave overhang, and grouped windows. Its three-story bays of open porches with metal railings, which curve back toward the building, on the second and third level are among the building's most distinguishing features.[7] The building, whose name is thought to derive from Wilburn's middle name,[8] once expressed the bourgeois aspirations of Atlanta's rising middle class. Because of its distinctive features, it is a locally well-known historic landmark, and it is still functioning as multiresidential housing.

Piedmont Park Apartments at 266 11th Street in Atlanta is an outstanding example of an early-twentieth-century apartment building in the

leader, solicited the younger Wilburn's help in actualizing the plans.[4] In an article describing the beginning of the 1909 school year, the *Atlanta Constitution* celebrated the building, scheduled to open later that year: "The design was created by Mrs. Alonzo Richardson, and was carried into effect by Miss Leila Ross Wilburn, an architect of Atlanta."[5] It was a two-story structure in the craftsman style, with a central two-story bay and two horizontal, low-arched front porches that wrapped around the sides. These features enhanced interior light and cross-ventilation. A rendering of the front elevation of this one-story craftsman style structure was published in the school's yearbook, *The Arsenal*, in 1919, as shown in Figure App.1.[6] The building has since been demolished.

The Rosslyn Apartments, a three-story apartment building constructed in 1913 in the craftsman style, is an outstanding and idiosyncratic example of a Wilburn commission that still stands today, at 344 Ponce de Leon Avenue, on a major Atlanta thoroughfare (see Fig. App.2). The craftsman architectural details of this three-story apartment building

FIGURE APP.2. The Rosslyn Apartments, built in 1913 in Atlanta at 344 Ponce de Leon Avenue. Photo taken in 2017.

FIGURE App.3. Piedmont Park Apartments at 266 11th Street in Atlanta. The building is on the National Register of Historic Places.

eclectic style. It is an elegant three-story brick building built with twenty-two units that had prominent porches on the front of the building and a combination of craftsman and Tudor style details. Rear balconies overlooking Piedmont Park provided private outdoor spaces and grand views of one of Atlanta's largest and most beautiful public parks. The apartments were renovated into condominiums in 2000, and at that time two new buildings were added, creating a residential complex of three buildings with a central courtyard. The complex was renamed "The Wilburn House Condominiums," in recognition of the architect who designed the original apartment building. In 2001 the Wilburn House was awarded an Atlanta Urban Design Commission Award for Excellence in Historic Preservation.[9] Figure App.3 shows the exterior of this historic building.

The Devonshire and Chatham Court Apartments, a three-story, red-brick apartment building, was constructed in 1918, soon after the Atlanta Fire of 1917. It was an example of a hotel-style apartment building, featuring a single entrance and apartment entrances from a central corridor.[10] With a simple rectilinear massing and a plain façade, it offered economical housing for urban residents in a convenient Midtown location. Located on Piedmont Avenue in the Midtown Historic District, the apartments have been renovated into attractive condominiums and renamed Piedmont and 3rd Condominiums.

Seven listings in the *Manufacturers Record* published between 1910 and 1922 document the construction of eight additional apartment buildings, a church, and a realty company headquarters designed by Wilburn. A

FIGURE APP.4. The Devonshire and Chatham Court Apartments (now known as Piedmont and 3rd Condominiums) are in the Midtown Historic District in Atlanta. Photo taken in 2017.

listing in the *Industrial Index* documents the renovation of a hotel and retail stores, with additions, with Wilburn as the architect.

The June 30, 1910, *Manufacturers Record* announces that "J. W. and Paul G. Goldsmith, East Lake, Ga., had plans prepared by Leila Ross Wilburn" for "two six-family apartment buildings; brick veneer and stone; vapor heat; electric and gas lighting; cost within $55,000; construction by day labor" (p. 60). These buildings have been identified by researcher John Wells as the Lambdin Apartment Building.[11] They are the first apartment

buildings known to have been designed by Wilburn. There are no known records identifying their location.

The February 5, 1914, *Manufacturers Record* announces, "E. Ragland let contract to Fulton County Home Builders, Atlanta, to erect two 2-story brick veneer apartment-houses at 211 Moreland Ave. and 433 Euclid Ave.; cost $18,000; Leila Ross Wilburn, Archt., Atlanta" (p. 78).

The May 27, 1915, *Manufacturers Record* announces, "Mrs. Field let contract to W. H. S. Hamilton, Atlanta, to erect apartment-house; brick veneer; stone veranda foundation; tile and tar and gravel roof; tile bath and porch floors; furnace heat; cost about $6500; Leila Ross Wilburn, Arch." (p. 50). The same issue lists Wilburn as the architect for the Sutherland Realty Company Story Building in the Kirkwood neighborhood between Atlanta and Decatur (p. 52). The estimated cost for this building was $4,000. Neither of these buildings has been located.

The December 6, 1917, *Manufacturers Record* announces, "W. H. Turner let contract to W. H. S. Hamilton, Decatur, Ga., to erect proposed 2-story brick-veneer 4-family apartment-house; plans by Leila Ross Wilburn, 305 Peters Bldg., Atlanta, call for terra-cotta trim; composition shingle and tar and gravel roof; tile bath floors; 8 hardwood floors; electric lights; steam heat; 4 fireplaces; cost $12,000" (p. 92). The location of this building on Parkway Drive in Atlanta has been confirmed. The building is still in use today.

The June 5, 1918, *Industrial Index* announced the creation of a large hotel building, also with Wilburn as architect. The ad read, "Jones-Ramspeck Co. will add one story and part of first story to three existing store buildings; building will contain, when finished, two stores and hotel lobby, dining room and kitchen on third floor, and 17 rooms and six baths and verandas on second floor. Miss Leila Ross Wilburn, 305 Peters Bldg., Atlanta, Ga., is the architect." This building has not been located, and we have no additional information about this project.

The December 15, 1921, *Manufacturers Record* announces, "Mrs. Nora G. Webb, Imperial Hotel, will erect $25,000 apartment house; 100x40 ft.; concrete and brick veneer; tile and asphalt roof; hardwood floors; interior tile; ventilators; Leila Ross Wilburn, Archt.; Webb Const. Co., Contr." (p. 91). This historic apartment building on Highland Avenue in the Inman Park neighborhood is also mentioned in the notice of "Buildings Proposed and Being Erected" in the October 30, 1921, edition of the *Atlanta Constitution*: "Webb Construction Company, Forsyth building, city, has plans just completed for a $25,000 eight-family apartment building for Highland Avenue, near Colquitt avenue. Two stories, brick veneer walls, tile and asphalt roof, tile bath floors, hardwood floors in main rooms, steam head. Size of building 100x36 feet. Construction to be started at once. Leila Ross Wilburn, architect." The building is still in use in this historic neighborhood in Atlanta.

The March 23, 1922, *Manufacturers Record* announces, "Mrs. Nora G. Webb will erect apartment house at 591–5 Highland Ave.; 115x90 ft.; 18 apartments; concrete, brick and stucco; asphalt roof; hardwood floors; ornamental terra cotta; interior tile; mail chutes; steam heat; L. R. Wilburn, Archt.; Webb Const. Co., Contr." (p. 78).

In addition to the custom design commissions described in this appendix, Wilburn served as a draftsperson in support of the war effort of the United States during both World War I and World War II. Personnel records of her employment are preserved in government archives, but no known record of specific drawings made during either period survives.

From 1917 to 1918, Wilburn served in the Army civilian service at Fort McPherson, Georgia, as a draftsperson for the War Department. According to her personnel records, her drafting duties at Fort McPherson included architectural drafting and listing materials. During World War II, Wilburn re-enlisted as a civilian, serving from 1942 to 1945 in Tampa, Fla., and then in Washington, D.C. She served as a draftsperson in Tampa in 1942–1943, and she was then promoted to a senior draftsperson position in Washington, D.C., where she worked from 1943 to 1945. Personnel records indicate that in Tampa her work was primarily the development of maps, and in her position in Washington, D.C., she was responsible for developing architectural plans and construction drawings for utilitarian structures.[12]

NOTES

FOREWORD

1. Downing, *Cottage Residences*, i.

2. Keith Publishing Co. advertisement in *Ladies Home Journal*, July 1901, 23; J. H. Daverman & Son advertisement in *Ladies Home Journal*, March 1907, 50; E. W. Stillwell's advertisement in *House and Garden*, April 1911, 289.

3. *Industrial Index*, 1914; *Atlanta Constitution*, May 2, 1915, 6.

4. "Fighting Ready-Cut Houses," *Gulf Coast Lumberman* 4, no. 9 (Aug. 1, 1916): 24 ; "Bought Plan Book Systems," *Gulf Coast Lumberman* 3, no. 18 (Dec. 15, 1915): 14 ; Roark, "Make Lots of Little Plans: The R. M. Williamson House Plan Books," 25.

5. "Correspondence: Advertised House Plans and Their Estimates of Cost," *Carpentry and Building* 31, no. 9 (Sept. 1, 1907): 294.

6. Wilburn, *Southern Homes and Bungalows*, 2.

7. Wilburn, *Brick and Colonial Homes*, 2.

8. Wilburn, *Southern Homes and Bungalows*, 2.

9. Margaret Culbertson, "Airing Out: Sleeping Porches and the Turn-of-the-Century Fresh-Air-Sleeping Movement," 44–46; C. M. d'Enville, "Outdoor Sleeping for the Well Man," *Country Life in America*, May 1909, 44; T. E. Whittlesey, "Building a Sleeping-porch," *House and Garden*, January 1910, 44.

10. Lewis, *Babbit*, 95.

INTRODUCTION

1. Llewellyn Willet Wilburn, unpublished family history manuscript, 1978.

2. According to information in the 1895–1908 editions of the *Atlanta City Directory* (Atlanta, Ga.: Foote and Davies), Joseph Wilburn worked as a clerk with Inman, Smith, & Co., a textile manufacturer and distributor of dry goods, and then as a bookkeeper in the same firm. He then worked for Cotton States B & S Co., and finally for Binders Frame Manufacturing Co.

3. Agnes Scott Institute was renamed Agnes Scott College in 1906 (Garrett, *Atlanta and Its Environs*, 2:196). Llewellyn graduated from Agnes Scott College; Alice attended but did not graduate from the college.

4. Boykin interview with Lib Kennedy, 1993.

5. As discussed in chapter 1 of this book, an architectural apprenticeship was a common educational path for individuals who wanted to become architects (particularly residential architects) through training and experience, rather than by pursuing an academic degree.

6. This date is confirmed by a listing in the 1908 *Atlanta City Directory* that reads, "Miss L. R. Welburn, 305 Peters Building." "Welburn" is almost certainly a misspelled listing of Wilburn, since Wilburn used this address for many years. Information about Wilburn's employment in the Army civilian service comes from copies of personnel records provided to Susan M. Hunter by the National Personnel Records Center (Civilian Personnel Records), National Archives and Records Administration, St. Louis, Mo. On her civilian personnel records, completed in 1943, Wilburn lists 1907–1909 as her years with B. R. Padgett & Sons, but the earlier documentation suggests that the two-year period of employment at Padgett began in 1906.

7. For additional information about Wilburn's custom commissions in the early years of her architectural practice, see the appendix.

8. Clarke, *The Story of Decatur, 1823–1899*, p. 6.

9. *The DeKalb New Era*, June 13, 1912, p. 1.

10. Garrett, *Atlanta and Its Environs*, 2:834. The growth of Atlanta during Wilburn's career receives extended attention in Garrett's second volume.

11. Ibid.

12. *The DeKalb News Era*, June 13, 1912, p. 1.

13. Lynn Speno, "McDonough–Adams–Kings Highway Historic District," National Register of Historic Places Registration Form, November 5, 2013, on file at the Historic Preservation Division, Georgia Department of Natural Resources, Stockbridge, Ga.

14. Ibid.

15. Miriam Mathura, "MAK Neighborhood History" (unpublished manuscript, 1986), DeKalb History Center, Decatur, Ga. 115 Adams Street is the street address given for Alice Frierson on Leila Ross Wilburn's civilian personnel records on forms dated 1943.

16. Lib Frierson Kennedy, Wilburn's niece, conversation with Sarah Boykin, 1993.

17. Boykin interview with Jean Kennedy Dantzler, 2017.

18. Joseph Wilburn IV, conversation with Sarah Boykin about Joseph Wilburn's father, an Atlanta architect, in August 2017.

19. See "Leila Ross Wilburn, Architect, 2003 Inductee," Georgia Women of Achievement, 2016, https://www.georgiawomen.org/leila-ross-wilburn.

CHAPTER 1. A Man's Profession, a Woman's Domain

1. More than eighty photographs of houses that had already been constructed using Wilburn's designs were published in Wilburn's first plan book. The *Manufacturers Record*, a publication of the Southern Association of Science and Industry that announced current construction projects, also lists houses designed by Wilburn.

2. See the *DeKalb New Era*, June 13, 1912, p. 1.

3. In Wilburn's first plan book, every mail-order house plan offered for sale is shown with a photograph of a completed design. In later plan books, some stock plans are illustrated with drawings of the exterior, others with photographs.

4. Wilburn, *Southern Homes and Bungalows*, p. 1.

5. Ibid., p. 26.

6. Ibid., p. 3.

7. *Year Book of the Atlanta Real Estate Board* (Atlanta, 1922), pp. 67–69.

8. Ibid.

9. Wilburn was one of many exhibitors at the show. The *Atlanta Constitution* of May 7, 1922, stated, "Leila Ross Wilburn will give a complete set of architect's drawings, containing working drawings and elevations, all ready to put into the hands of the builder." The paper also ran a Wilburn ad and mentioned a special discount Wilburn offered to expo attendees for purchase of her latest plan book, *Brick and Colonial Homes*.

10. *Year Book of the Atlanta Real Estate Board*, p. 1.

11. Although the yearbook has many advertisements from contractors, suppliers, realtors, builders, and others in the housing industry, there is only one other advertisement for stock houses, by "The Minter Homes Co." (p. 94).

12. Wilburn, *Ideal Homes of Today*, p. 2.

13. Wilburn, *Southern Homes and Bungalows*, p. 27.

14. Information about Wilburn's employment history, along with a description of her work, was obtained from documents Wilburn completed when applying for the Army civilian service in 1942. On the applications she wrote under "duties and responsibilities" of her office, "drawing complete plans for

houses, apartments, churches, business buildings, writing specifications—listing materials." Copies were provided to Susan M. Hunter by the National Personnel Records Center (Civilian Personnel Records), National Archives and Records Administration, St. Louis, Mo.

15. Wilburn, *Brick and Colonial Homes*, p. 2.

16. Wilburn, *Small Low-Cost Homes for the South*, p. 2.

17. Wilburn, *Brick and Colonial Homes*, p. 2.

18. Cole, *From Tipi to Skyscraper*, p. 75. MIT, Cornell, and the University of Illinois were among the first architectural schools. As land-grant universities, they were open to men and women.

19. Prior to 1920, Georgia, like many other states, had no academic or state professional license requirements restricting one from practicing architecture.

20. Oral interview in 1993 with Elizabeth Frierson (Lib) Kennedy, Alice Frierson's daughter and Wilburn's niece.

21. The exact dates for Wilburn's employment at B. R. Padgett & Sons are not known. Wilburn provided conflicting information in her employment history on the personnel records cited in note 14, which are the only known records. In 1943, when she was applying for a promotion from her position in Tampa to a position as a "senior engineering draftsman" in Washington, D.C., she stated that she worked for the company from 1907 to 1908. Another document, from 1942, lists her dates of employment with B. R. Padgett as "9-07-9-09." However, she was listed in the *Atlanta City Directory* of 1908, although her name was misspelled; the listing reads "Miss Leila R. Welburn, Leila R. Miss, architect, 305 Peters bldg r Decatur Ga" (see *Atlanta City Directory* [Atlanta, Ga.: Foote and Davies, 1908], p. 1331). We date the beginning of Wilburn's practice to 1908, following the *Atlanta City Directory*, because this source was published during the time in question. It appears that Wilburn worked for B. R. Padgett & Sons for two years, so we believe that Wilburn worked for B. R. Padgett & Sons from 1906 to 1908, during the two years before she opened her own office.

22. Advertisement for B. R. Padgett & Sons included in the 1908 *Atlanta City Directory* in an unfolioed insert between pages 369 and 370.

23. Berkeley and McQuaid, eds., *Architecture: A Place for Women*, pp. 254–55.

24. Margaret W. Love, "Ellamae Ellis League, FAIA," master's thesis, Georgia Institute of Technology, 1981, provides the most complete documentation of League's life and career.

25. Berkeley and McQuaid, eds., *Architecture: A Place for Women*, pp. 179–80.

26. Cole, *From Tipi to Skyscraper*, pp. 78–80.

27. Much of the above information about Ellamae Ellis League and Jean League Newton was provided by Newton's daughter, Suzy Newton, in 2017. In 1970, according to Newton, the Harvard Graduate School of Design changed her mother's degree, which she had earned in 1944, from a B. Arch. to a M. Arch., stating that she had, in fact, earned a graduate degree at that time.

28. Berkeley and McQuaid, eds., *Architecture: A Place for Women*, pp. 179–80.

29. Bamby Ray, "Ellamae Ellis League (1899–1991)," *New Georgia Encyclopedia*, 31 May 2016.

30. Due to the cost of architectural design services and the time required to produce a custom design, architects for the most part were not as successful as builders in supplying economical house plans for middle-class residences.

31. Reiff, *Houses from Books*, pp. 149, 309–19. Both lists were offered as extensive but not comprehensive accounts of all plan book publishers. Reiff's book is one of the most important sources on the history of the plan book tradition, with a comprehensive history and survey of this American tradition, accompanied by hundreds of illustrations from published sources offered for residential design and construction from 1738 to 1950.

32. Margaret Culbertson uses the term "house catalogue" for "catalogues selling house plans," and the term "ready-cut house catalogues" to "refer to catalogues selling building components for entire houses." Culbertson, *Texas Houses Built by the Book*, p. 17. We use the term "plan books" to refer to Wilburn's publications of mail-order house plans because this is the term that Wilburn herself used for these publications.

33. Jennings, "Leila Ross Wilburn: Plan-Book Architect," p. 10.

34. Reiff, *Houses from Books*, pp. 149–50.

35. Culbertson, *Texas Houses Built by the Book*, pp. 23, 27–29.

36. Ibid., p. 35.

37. Ibid., p. 23.

38. Ibid., pp. 17–18.

39. In *The Comfortable House*, Alan Gowans provided a thorough description of many sources for mail-order house plans and mail-order houses, the services each provided, and the ways in which they contrasted with traditional architectural services. In *America's Favorite Homes*, Robert Schweitzer and Michael W. R. Davis described mail-order house companies, which were located throughout the United States.

40. Jennings, "Leila Ross Wilburn: Plan-Book Architect," p. 10.

41. Schweitzer and Davis, *America's Favorite Homes*, p. 63.

42. Frank Daniel, "Atlanta Women Have Man-Size Jobs," *Atlanta Journal*, August 24, 1924, p. 7.

43. Wilburn, *Ideal Homes of Today*, p. 2.

44. Wilburn, *Brick and Colonial Homes*, p. 2.

45. *The Industrial Index*, Feb. 24, 1914.

46. See the appendix to this book for more information about Wilburn's service during the two world wars.

47. Federal employment personnel records, National Personnel Records Center (Civilian Personnel Records), National Archives and Records Administration, St. Louis, Mo.

48. Smith, "Women Architects in Atlanta, 1895–1979," p. 86.

49. Wilburn, *Ideal Homes of Today*, p. 2.

50. *Atlanta Constitution*, October 30, 1921, p. 6.

51. Wilburn's first plan book provided little information about her plan book business, her business practice, or the cost for drawings, etc.; such information was included in later plan books.

52. Wilburn, *Brick and Colonial Homes*, p. 2.

53. Ibid.

54. Ibid.

55. Wilburn, *Brick and Colonial Homes*, p. 2.

56. *Ideal Homes of Today*, p. 8; *Brick and Colonial Homes*, pp. 23, 25, 29, 39, 10, 3.

57. Wilburn, *Ideal Homes of Today*, p. 29.

58. Ibid., p. 2.

59. Ibid.

60. Wilburn, *Homes in Good Taste*.

61. Wilburn, *Ideal Homes of Today*, p. 2.

62. Wilburn, *Brick and Colonial Homes*, p. 2.

63. Ibid.

64. Wilburn, *Ranch and Colonial Homes*, p. 1.

65. See Reiff and Culbertson's books for more information on these companies.

66. Wilburn, *One-Story Houses*.

67. See Wilburn, *Brick and Colonial Homes*, p. 2.

68. The correspondence between Wilburn and her client is part of the Leila Ross Wilburn Collection in the Kenan Research Center in the Atlanta History Center.

69. The Leila Ross Wilburn Collection in the Kenan Research Center at the Atlanta History Center includes drawings and correspondence that document houses built and plans ordered from individuals in Georgia, Alabama, Florida, Oklahoma, North Carolina, South Carolina, and Mississippi.

CHAPTER 2. Southern Comfort, American Style

1. Wilburn, *Ideal Homes of Today*, p. 2.

2. The first five plan books were published from 1914 until ca. 1930, with no exact publication dates known for the third, fourth, and fifth plan books.

3. Many of Wilburn's plan book houses have been documented in several National Register Historic Districts in the Atlanta area. For example, they can be found in the Ansley Park Historic District, Candler Park Historic District, Druid Hills Historic District, and Midtown Historic District. They also contribute to the architectural and historical significance of the South Candler St./Agnes Scott College Historic District and the McDonough–Adams St.–King's Highway (MAK) Historic District in Decatur, Ga. Wilburn also designed several apartment buildings in the Midtown Historic District, as described in the appendix to this volume.

4. Wilburn, *Southern Homes and Bungalows*, p. 3.

5. Although the technology for central air conditioning systems existed in the early twentieth century, it was not a common feature in houses in much of the South until after the economic boom of the late 1940s. It became more afford-able and thus more common by the 1960s.

6. McAlester, *A Field Guide to American Houses*, p. 406.

7. The craftsman style enjoyed national popularity as an early modern house type, particularly for the American bungalow, but the prairie style was primarily popular in the Midwest, where it had its origins. There are no known Wilburn plan book houses featuring the prairie style.

8. McAlester, *A Field Guide to American Houses*, p. 406.

9. Clark, *The American Family Home*, pp. 162–63.

10. Wilburn, *Southern Homes and Bungalows*, p. 3.

11. McAlester, *A Field Guide to American Houses*, pp. 567–69.

12. Wilburn, *Southern Homes and Bungalows*, p. 3.

13. McAlester, *A Field Guide to American Houses*, p. 406.

14. Ibid., p. 568.

15. Wilburn, *Brick and Colonial Homes*, p. 1.

16. Wright, *Moralism and the Model Home*, p. 134. Wright cites *The House Beautiful*, the *Ladies' Home Journal*, *Cosmopolitan*, and *The Craftsman* as publica-tions that advocated for housing reforms.

17. Wilburn, *Southern Homes and Bungalows*, p. 47.

18. Ibid., p. 44.

19. Ibid., p. 90.

20. Ibid., p. 28.

21. Wilburn, *Brick and Colonial Homes*, p. 2.

22. Wright, *Moralism and the Model Home*, p. 245.

23. Wilburn, *Southern Homes and Bungalows*, p. 39.

24. Ibid., p. 3.

25. Ibid., p. 13.

26. Wright, *Moralism and the Model Home*, p. 242.

27. Wilburn, *Southern Homes and Bungalows*, p. 50.

28. Ibid., p. 41.

29. Clark, *The American Family Home*, p. 132.

30. Wilburn, *Southern Homes and Bungalows*, p. 47.

31. Wilburn, *Brick and Colonial Homes*, p. 26.

32. Wilburn, *Ideal Homes of Today*, p. 39.

33. McAlester, *A Field Guide to American Houses*, p. 568.

34. Ibid., pp. 406–7.

35. Ibid., p. 406.

36. Ibid., p. 407.

37. McAlester, *A Field Guide to American Houses*, p. 14.

38. Ibid., pp. 448–54.

39. Wilburn, *Homes in Good Taste*, p. 8.

40. Ibid., p. 49.

41. Wilburn, *Brick and Colonial Homes*, p. 40.

42. Ibid., p. 38.

43. McAlester, *A Field Guide to American Houses*, pp. 408–14.

44. Wilburn, *Ideal Homes of Today*, p. 8.

45. Ibid., p. 19.

46. Wilburn, *Brick and Colonial Homes*, p. 37.

47. Ibid., p. 13.

48. Wilburn, *Homes in Good Taste*, p. B.

49. Ibid., p. 26.

50. Loose pages from this plan book are included in the Leila Ross Wilburn Collection in the Kenan Research Center at the Atlanta History Center.

51. Wilburn, *New Homes of Quality*, p. 35.

52. Wilburn, *Brick and Colonial Homes*, p. 2.

53. Clark, *The American Family Home*, p. 132.

54. Wilburn, *Brick and Colonial Homes*, p. 2.

55. Ibid.

56. Wilburn, *Ideal Homes of Today*, p. 41.

57. According to Jan Jennings, "two-family houses as a way to promote home ownership were popular in the trade press" during the first two decades of the twentieth century" ("Leila Ross Wilburn: Plan-Book Architect," p. 14).

58. Wilburn, *Southern Homes and Bungalows*, p. 55.

59. Wilburn, *Homes in Good Taste*, p. 27.

60. Wilburn, *Brick and Colonial Homes*, p. 12.

61. Wilburn, *New Homes of Quality*, p. 48.

62. Ibid., p. 49.

63. See the appendix to this book for more information about documented custom commissions.

64. Wilburn, *Brick and Colonial Homes*, p. 39.

CHAPTER 3. From 1930s Small to 1950s Ranch

Drawings for each of the seven houses shown in this chapter (as examples of houses designed from plan designs in Wilburn's later plan books) are located in the Leila Ross Wilburn Collection in the Kenan Research Center at the Atlanta History Center. These drawings identify the client, location/address, and plan design number for each house.

1. Wilburn's later plan books include *Small Low-Cost Homes for the South*, *Sixty Good New Homes*, *Ranch and Colonial Homes*, and *Bran-New Homes*. Interestingly, the plan design number for each house in Wilburn's last four plan books correspond to the square footage for that particular house, including porches.

2. The "minimal traditional house" is the term used by Virginia McAlester in *A Field Guide to American Houses* to refer to this small house type, which was prevalent from 1935 to 1950. See pp. 586–95. In 2002, the Georgia State Historic Preservation Office in the Historic Preservation Division of the Georgia Department of Natural Resources published a document describing this house type and its historical importance in the development of mid-twentieth-century suburbs in Georgia. See "The American Small House," Historic Preservation Division, Georgia Department of Natural Resources, http://georgiashpo.org /sites/default/files/hpd/pdf/AmericanSmallHouse.pdf.

3. *Sixty Good New Homes*, *Ranch and Colonial Homes*, and *Bran-New Homes* each offered a statement on the first page that read, "The group of attractive and practical homes illustrated in this book were especially designed for the average American family." Although it is not clear exactly what Wilburn meant by "the average American family," she likely, given the size of her plan book

houses during this period and the continued demand for houses for middle class households, was referring to both income and size. Her houses continued to be economical, and most had from two to three bedrooms, which probably would have been adequate for a couple with several children, i.e. a middle-income household of four or five family members.

4. The Leila Ross Wilburn Collection in the Kenan Research Center at the Atlanta History Center holds many of the sets of drawings for houses that were designed during this later period.

5. Wright, *Building the Dream*, p. 240.

6. Ibid., p. 240.

7. McAlester, *A Field Guide to American Houses*, pp. 586–89.

8. Ibid., pp. 586–88.

9. *Principles of Planning Small Houses*, p. 3.

10. McAlester, *A Field Guide to American Houses*, pp. 588–89.

11. Ibid., p. 588.

12. Although the exact date of publication is not known, we believe that *Small Low-Cost Homes for the South* was published after the 1934 Federal Housing Act to offer minimal traditional house designs as well as other smaller houses for homeowners.

13. Wilburn, *Small Low-Cost Homes for the South*, p. 1.

14. McAlester, *A Field Guide to American Houses*, pp. 586–87.

15. Wilburn, *Small Low-Cost Homes for the South*, p. 1.

16. *Principles of Planning Small Houses*, p. 5.

17. Ibid., p. 3.

18. Original drawings are in the Leila Ross Wilburn Collection of the Kenan Research Center at the Atlanta History Center.

19. Wilburn, *Small Low-Cost Homes for the South*, p. 41.

20. Ibid., p. 19.

21. Original drawings for plan design no. 1341 for C. E. Beem are located in the Leila Ross Wilburn Collection of the Kenan Research Center at the Atlanta History Center.

22. Wilburn, *Small Low-Cost Homes for the South*, p. 34.

23. Ibid., p. 40.

24. The correspondence is held in the Leila Ross Wilburn collection in the Kenan Research Center at the Atlanta History Center.

25. Wilburn, *Sixty Good New Homes*, p. 2.

26. Although the exact date is not known, *Sixty Good New Homes* likely was published before 1942. However, it may have been published soon after Wilburn returned from the Civilian Service (in 1945).

27. McAlester, *A Field Guide to American Houses*, p. 600.

28. Ibid., pp. 600–603.

29. Wilburn, *Sixty Good New Homes*, p. 26.

30. The Leila Ross Wilburn Collection in the Kenan Research Center at the Atlanta History Center contains a number of drawings that were produced for contractor J. O. Anderson for houses built in the Atlanta area.

31. Wilburn, *Sixty Good New Homes*, p. 25.

32. Ibid.

33. Ibid., p. 3.

34. This information is from Wilburn's personnel records. More information about Wilburn's civilian service in both World War I and World War II can be found in the appendix to this volume.

35. Correspondence in the Leila Ross Wilburn Collection in the Kenan Research Center at the Atlanta History Center documents two orders for drawings and specifications, in addition to the letter from Cushing, Ok., already discussed. A May 1948 letter from Baker, Fla., requested plan design no. 438 in *Homes in Good Taste*, and a November 1949 letter from Albemarle, N.C., requested a set of reverse plans for plan design no. 3155 in *Sixty Good New Homes*.

36. Sullivan, Reed, and Fedor, *The Ranch House in Georgia*.

37. Hayden, *Building Suburbia*, p. 132.

38. McAlester, *A Field Guide to American Houses*, p. 602

39. Ibid., pp. 597–602. Photographs of a variety of ranch houses built with different rooflines throughout the United States are shown in ibid., pp. 604–11.

40. Ibid., pp. 602–3.

41. Ibid., pp. 694–699.

42. Wilburn, *Ranch and Colonial Homes*, p. 9.

43. Ibid., p. 3.

44. Ibid., p. 15.

45. Ibid., p. 8.

46. Ibid., p. 50.

47. Although the house as built does not exactly match the plan design as shown in the plan book, the drawings for this house identified it as plan design no. 2268.

48. We date this plan book based on 1960 correspondence with a prospective client in Hamilton, Ala., held in the Leila Ross Wilburn Collection in the Kenan Research Center at the Atlanta History Center, in which Wilburn remarked that she was preparing to publish her next plan book, following the publication of *Ranch and Colonial Homes* (which had been cited earlier by the client).

49. Wilburn, *Ranch and Colonial Homes*, p. 39.

50. McAlester, *A Field Guide to American Houses*, pp. 613–14.

51. Wilburn, *Bran-New Homes*, p. 2.

52. Ibid., p. 18.

53. Ibid.

54. Wilburn, *Bran-New Homes*, p. 20.

55. Ibid., p. 7.

CHAPTER 4. Learning from Wilburn in the Twenty-First Century

1. In addition to the authors, Catherine W. Bishir, Robert M. Craig, Jan Jennings, and David Ramsey are among the individuals who have contributed information and insights about Wilburn's architectural legacy. Elizabeth Frierson (Lib) Kennedy, Wilburn's niece, also made significant contributions, including providing historical information about the Wilburn family and her beloved "Aunt Lee."

2. The Leila Ross Wilburn Collection in the Kenan Research Center at the Atlanta History Center has more than three hundred sets of drawings. The collection includes drawings of houses designed for clients in Georgia, Florida, Mississippi, Alabama, and North Carolina. Wilburn-designed houses built

in North Carolina also are documented in Catherine W. Bishir, "Leila Ross Wilburn, 1885–1967," *North Carolina Architects and Builders: A Biographical Dictionary*, North Carolina State University Libraries, http://ncarchitects.lib.ncsu.edu/people/P000546.

3. Wilburn, *Brick and Colonial Homes*, p. 2.

4. Ibid., p. 25.

5. Wilburn, *Southern Homes and Bungalows*, p. 14.

6. Wilburn, *Brick and Colonial Homes*, p. 31.

7. Wilburn, *Ideal Homes of Today*, p. 11.

8. Wilson and Dawson Architects of Atlanta, Ga., were the architects for the project.

9. After the historic rehabilitation project was completed, the house and owners were honored with a 2016 Preservation Award for Outstanding Rehabilitation from the Athens-Clarke Heritage Foundation, Athens, Ga.

10. Wilburn, *Small Low-Cost Homes for the South*, p. 49.

APPENDIX

1. According to the city of Atlanta's Urban Design Commission, "Between 1900 and 1920, Wilburn was aware of the nationwide boom in urban apartment construction. She designed 30 apartment complexes in Atlanta during those years including the Rosslyn on Ponce de Leon. The apartments ranged in size from four to twenty-two units." "Piedmont Park Apartments," Atlanta Urban Design Commission, https://www.atlantaga.gov/government/departments/planning-community-development/office-of-zoning-development/urban-design-commission/piedmont-park-apartments.

2. See Smith, "Women Architects in Atlanta," p. 90.

3. Ballentine, *The Woodward Story*, p. 45.

4. For Richardson's activities in the community, see "Atlanta's First Woman of the Year Dies," *Atlanta Constitution*, April 30, 1946, p. 13. Richardson was named Woman of the Year in 1936.

5. *Atlanta Constitution*, September 9, 1909, p. 5.

6. A photo taken at a later date appears in Ballentine, *The Woodward Story*, p. 44.

7. *Atlanta's Lasting Landmarks*, p. 81.

8. Ibid.

9. Information about this building is taken from "Piedmont Park Apartments," Urban Design Commission, City of Atlanta, https://www.atlantaga.gov/government/departments/planning-community-development/office-of-zoning-development/urban-design-commission/piedmont-park-apartments.

10. "Piedmont and Third," Easements Atlanta, http://easementsatlanta.org/portfolio-items/piedmont-and-third/.

11. Correspondence with Sarah Boykin, January 28, 1994.

12. Information in this paragraph comes from copies of Wilburn's personnel records provided to Susan M. Hunter by the National Personnel Records Center (Civilian Personnel Records), National Archives and Records Administration, St. Louis, Mo.

BIBLIOGRAPHY

Publications by Leila Ross Wilburn are listed separately on p. vii.

Allaback, Sarah. *The First American Women Architects*. Urbana: University of
    Illinois Press, 2008.
"The American Small House." Historic Preservation Division, Georgia
    Department of Natural Resources. http://www.georgiashpo.org/sites/default
    /files/hpd/pdf/AmericanSmallHouse_0.pdf.
Atlanta Historic Resources Workbook. Atlanta Urban Design Commission, 1981.
Atlanta's Lasting Landmarks. Atlanta Urban Design Commission, 1987.
Ballentine, Robert D. *The Woodward Story: A History of Georgia Military/
    Woodward Academy, 1900–1990*. College Park, Ga.: Woodward Academy, 1990.
Berkeley, Ellen Perry, and Matilda McQuaid, eds. *Architecture: A Place for
    Women*. Washington, D.C.: Smithsonian Institution Press, 1989.
Bishir, Catherine W. "Leila Ross Wilburn, 1885–1967." *North Carolina Architects
    and Builders: A Biographical Dictionary*, North Carolina State University
    Libraries, http://ncarchitects.lib.ncsu.edu/people/P000546.
Clark, Clifford Edward, Jr. *The American Family Home, 1800–1960*. Chapel Hill:
    University of North Carolina Press, 1986.
Clarke, Caroline McKinney. *The Story of Decatur, 1823–1899*. Decatur, Ga.: City
    of Decatur, 1973.
Cloues, Richard, "House Types." *New Georgia Encyclopedia*, August 23,
    2013,http://www.georgiaencyclopedia.org/articles/arts-culture
    /house-types.
Cole, Doris. *From Tipi to Skyscraper: A History of Women in Architecture*. Boston,
    Mass.: i press incorporated, 1973.

Craig, Robert M. "Leila Ross Wilburn (1885–1967)." *New Georgia Encyclopedia*,
    September 18, 2017. http://www.georgiaencyclopedia.org/articles/arts-culture
    /leila-ross-wilburn-1885-1967.
Culbertson, Margaret. "Airing Out: Sleeping Porches and the Turn-of-the-
    Century Fresh-Air-Sleeping Movement." *Cite: The Architecture and Design
    Review of Houston* (Spring 1996): 44–46.
———. *Texas Houses Built by the Book: The Use of Published Designs, 1850–1925*.
    College Station: Texas A&M University Press, 1999.
Downing, Andrew Jackson. *Cottage Residences*. New York: Wiley and Putnam, 1842.
Garrett, Franklin M. *Atlanta and Its Environs: A Chronicle of Its People and
    Events*, 2 vols. Athens: University of Georgia Press, 1969.
Gowans, Alan. *The Comfortable House: North American Suburban Architecture,
    1890–1930*. Cambridge, Mass.: MIT Press, 1987.
Hayden, Dolores. *Building Suburbia: Green Fields and Urban Growth, 1820–
    2000*. Reprint, New York: Vintage Books, 2004.
Hunter, Susan M. "Lady of the House: Leila Ross Wilburn, Architect." *Southern
    Homes* 7 no. 2 (March/April 1989): 136–40. (*See also* Smith, Susan Hunter.)
Jennings, Jan. "Leila Ross Wilburn: Plan-Book Architect." *Women's Art Journal*
    10, no. 1 (Spring/Summer 1989): 10–16.
Lewis, Sinclair. *Babbit*. New York: Grosset and Dunlap, 1922.
Love, Margaret W. "Ellamae Ellis League, FAIA." Master's thesis, Georgia
    Institute of Technology, 1981.
McAlester, Virginia Savage. *A Field Guide to American Houses: The Definitive
    Guide to Identifying and Understanding America's Domestic Architecture*. rev.
    ed. New York: Knopf, 2014.

Principles of Planning Small Houses. Washington, D.C.: Federal Housing Administration, 1936.

Ramsey, David Clifton. "The Architecture of Leila Ross Wilburn: An Investigation into the Plan Book Process and Ideology in Atlanta from 1910–1940." MA thesis, Georgia Institute of Technology, 1986.

Reiff, Daniel D. *Houses from Books: Treatises, Pattern Books, and Catalogs in American Architecture, 1738–1950: A History and Guide*. University Park: Pennsylvania State University Press, 2000.

Roark, Carol. "Make Lots of Little Plans: The R. M. Williamson House Plan Books." *Legacies: A History Journal for Dallas and North Central Texas* 9, no. 2 (Fall 1997): 24–29.

Roth, Leland M. *American Architecture: A History*. Boulder, Col.: Westview Press, 2001.

Schweitzer, Robert, and Michael W. R. Davis. *America's Favorite Homes: Mail-Order Catalogues as a Guide to Popular Early 20th-Century Houses*. Detroit, Mich.: Wayne State University Press, 1990.

Smith, Susan Hunter. "Women Architects in Atlanta, 1895–1979." *Atlanta Historical Journal* 23, no. 4 (Winter 1979–80): 85–108. (*See also* Hunter, Susan M.)

Stickley, Gustav, ed. *Craftsman Bungalows: 59 Homes from "The Craftsman."* New York: Dover, 1988.

Sullivan, Patrick, Mary Beth Reed, and Tracey Fedor. *The Ranch House in Georgia: Guidelines for Evaluation*. Stone Mountain, Ga.: New South Associates, 2010.

Torre, Susana, ed. *Women in American Architecture: A Historic and Contemporary Perspective*. New York: Whitney Library of Design, 1977.

Wright, Gwendolyn. *Building the Dream: A Social History of Housing in America*. New York: Pantheon Books, 1981.

———. *Moralism and the Model Home: Domestic Architecture and Cultural Conflict in Chicago, 1873–1913*. Chicago: University of Chicago Press, 1985.

ILLUSTRATION CREDITS

Fig. Int.1. Boykin Collection. Gift of Elizabeth (Lib) Frierson Kennedy / Fig. Int.2. Courtesy of Agnes Scott College, copyright 2014 / Fig. Int.4. William Bryan (Bill) Wilson, Kenan Research Center at the Atlanta History Center.

Fig. 1.1. Boykin Collection. Gift of Elizabeth (Lib) Frierson Kennedy / Fig. 1.2. Courtesy of Special Collections and Archives, McCain Library, Agnes Scott College / Fig. 1.3. Sarah J. Boykin, photographer / Fig. 1.4. Courtesy of Special Collections and Archives, McCain Library, Agnes Scott College / Fig. 1.5. Sarah J. Boykin, photographer / Fig. 1.6. Courtesy of Special Collections and Archives, McCain Library, Agnes Scott College / Fig. 1.7. Courtesy of Leonard Thibadeau / Fig. 1.8. Courtesy of Leonard Thibadeau / Fig. 1.9. Sarah J. Boykin, photographer / Fig. 1.10. Courtesy of Special Collections and Archives, McCain Library, Agnes Scott College / Fig. 1.11. Sarah J. Boykin, photographer / Fig. 1.12. Boykin Collection. Gift of Elizabeth (Lib) Frierson Kennedy / Fig. 1.13. Boykin Collection. Gift of Elizabeth (Lib) Frierson Kennedy / Fig. 1.14. Courtesy of Special Collections and Archives, McCain Library, Agnes Scott College / Fig. 1.15. Courtesy of Special Collections and Archives, McCain Library, Agnes Scott College / Fig. 1.16. Courtesy of Special Collections and Archives, McCain Library, Agnes Scott College / Fig. 1.17. Georgia State Archives / Fig. 1.18. Sarah J. Boykin / Fig. 1.19. Sarah J. Boykin / Fig. 1.20. Courtesy of Special Collections and Archives, McCain Library, Agnes Scott College / Fig. 1.21. Sarah J. Boykin / Fig. 1.22. Sarah J. Boykin.

Fig. 2.1. Sarah J. Boykin, photographer / Fig. 2.2. Sarah J. Boykin, photographer / Fig. 2.3. Courtesy of Special Collections and Archives, McCain Library, Agnes Scott College / Fig. 2.4. Sarah J. Boykin / Fig. 2.5. Sarah J. Boykin, photographer / Fig. 2.6. Courtesy of Special Collections and Archives, McCain Library, Agnes Scott College / Fig. 2.7. Courtesy of Special Collections and Archives, McCain Library, Agnes Scott College / Fig. 2.8. Sarah J. Boykin, photographer / Fig. 2.9. Courtesy of Special Collections and Archives, McCain Library, Agnes Scott College / Fig. 2.10. Sarah J. Boykin, photographer / Fig. 2.11. Courtesy of Special Collections and Archives, McCain Library, Agnes Scott College / Fig. 2.12. Sarah J. Boykin, photographer / Fig. 2.13. Courtesy of Special Collections and Archives, McCain Library, Agnes Scott College / Fig. 2.14. Sarah J. Boykin, photographer / Fig. 2.15. Courtesy of Special Collections and Archives, McCain Library, Agnes Scott College / Fig. 2.16. Courtesy of Special Collections and Archives, McCain Library, Agnes Scott College / Fig. 2.17. Sarah J. Boykin, photographer / Fig. 2.18. Courtesy of Special Collections and Archives, McCain Library, Agnes Scott College / Fig. 2.19. Courtesy of Special Collections and Archives, McCain Library, Agnes Scott College / Fig. 2.20. Sarah J. Boykin / Fig. 2.21. Sarah J. Boykin, photographer / Fig. 2.22. Sarah J. Boykin / Fig. 2.23. Sarah J. Boykin, photographer / Fig. 2.24. Sarah J. Boykin / Fig. 2.25. Sarah J. Boykin, photographer / Fig. 2.26. Sarah J. Boykin, photographer / Fig. 2.27. Courtesy of Special Collections and Archives, McCain Library, Agnes Scott College / Fig. 2.28. Courtesy of Special Collections and Archives, McCain Library, Agnes Scott College / Fig. 2.29. Sarah J. Boykin / Fig. 2.30. Daryl O'Hare Photography / Fig. 2.31. Sarah J. Boykin / Fig. 2.32. Sarah J. Boykin, photographer / Fig. 2.33. Sarah J. Boykin, photographer / Fig. 2.34. Sarah J. Boykin / Fig. 2.35. Sarah J. Boykin, photographer / Fig. 2.36. Sarah J. Boykin / Fig. 2.37. Sarah J. Boykin, photographer / Fig. 2.38.

Sarah J. Boykin / Fig. 2.39. Sarah J. Boykin, photographer / Fig. 2.40. Sarah J. Boykin / Fig. 2.41. Sarah J. Boykin, photographer / Fig. 2.42. Sarah J. Boykin / Fig. 2.43. Sarah J. Boykin, photographer / Fig. 2.44. Sarah J. Boykin, photographer / Fig. 2.45. Sarah J. Boykin, photographer / Fig. 2.46. Sarah J. Boykin / Fig. 2.47. Sarah J. Boykin, photographer / Fig. 2.48. Sarah J. Boykin, photographer / Fig. 2.49. Sarah J. Boykin / Fig. 2.50. Sarah J. Boykin, photographer / Fig. 2.51. Sarah J. Boykin, photographer / Fig. 2.52. Courtesy of Special Collections and Archives, McCain Library, Agnes Scott College / Fig. 2.53. Sarah J. Boykin, photographer / Fig. 2.54. Courtesy of Kenan Research Center at the Atlanta History Center / Fig. 2.55. Courtesy of Kenan Research Center at the Atlanta History Center / Fig. 2.56. Sarah J. Boykin, photographer / Fig. 2.57. Sarah J. Boykin, photographer / Fig. 2.58. Sarah J. Boykin / Fig. 2.59. Sarah J. Boykin, photographer / Fig. 2.60. Sarah J. Boykin, photographer / Fig. 2.61. Sarah J. Boykin, photographer / Fig. 2.62. Sarah J. Boykin, photographer / Fig. 2.63. Courtesy of Special Collections and Archives, McCain Library, Agnes Scott College / Fig. 2.64. Courtesy of Special Collections and Archives, McCain Library, Agnes Scott College / Fig. 2.65. Sarah J. Boykin / Fig. 2.66. Sarah J. Boykin, photographer / Fig. 2.67. Sarah J. Boykin, photographer / Fig. 2.68. Courtesy of Kenan Research Center at the Atlanta History Center / Fig. 2.69. Courtesy of Kenan Research Center at the Atlanta History Center / Fig. 2.70. Sarah J. Boykin / Fig. 2.71. Sarah J. Boykin, photographer.

Fig. 3.1. Sarah J. Boykin / Fig. 3.2. Sarah J. Boykin / Fig. 3.3. Sarah J. Boykin / Fig. 3.4. Sarah J. Boykin / Fig. 3.5. Daryl O'Hare Photography / Fig. 3.6. Sarah J. Boykin / Fig. 3.7. Sarah J. Boykin / Fig. 3.8. Daryl O'Hare Photography / Fig. 3.9. Sarah J. Boykin / Fig. 3.10. Sarah J. Boykin / Fig. 3.11. Courtesy of Special Collections and Archives, McCain Library, Agnes Scott College / Fig. 3.12. Courtesy of Special Collections and Archives, McCain Library, Agnes Scott College / Fig. 3.13. Courtesy of Kenan Research Center at the Atlanta History Center / Fig. 3.14. Daryl O'Hare Photography / Fig. 3.15. Courtesy of Kenan Research Center at the Atlanta History Center / Fig. 3.16. Daryl O'Hare Photography / Fig. 3.17. Courtesy of Kenan Research Center at the Atlanta History Center / Fig. 3.18. Daryl O'Hare Photography / Fig. 3.19. Courtesy of

Special Collections and Archives, McCain Library, Agnes Scott College / Fig. 3.20. Courtesy of Special Collections and Archives, McCain Library, Agnes Scott College / Fig. 3.21. Courtesy of Special Collections and Archives, McCain Library, Agnes Scott College / Fig. 3.22. Courtesy of Special Collections and Archives, McCain Library, Agnes Scott College / Fig. 3.23. Courtesy of Special Collections and Archives, McCain Library, Agnes Scott College / Fig. 3.24. Courtesy of Special Collections and Archives, McCain Library, Agnes Scott College / Fig. 3.25. Courtesy of Special Collections and Archives, McCain Library, Agnes Scott College / Fig. 3.26. Courtesy of Special Collections and Archives, McCain Library, Agnes Scott College / Fig. 3.27. Susan M. Hunter / Fig. 3.28. Sarah J. Boykin / Fig. 3.29. Sarah J. Boykin / Fig. 3.30. Sarah J. Boykin / Fig. 3.31. Sarah J. Boykin / Fig. 3.32. Sarah J. Boykin / Fig. 3.33. Sarah J. Boykin / Fig. 3.34. Daryl O'Hare Photography.

Fig. 4.1. Sarah J. Boykin, photographer / Fig. 4.2. Courtesy of Special Collections and Archives, McCain Library, Agnes Scott College / Fig. 4.3. Sarah J. Boykin, photographer / Fig. 4.4. Sarah J. Boykin, photographer / Fig. 4.5. Courtesy of Leisa Wray / Fig. 4.6. Courtesy of Leisa Wray / Fig. 4.7. Sarah J. Boykin / Fig. 4.8. Sarah J. Boykin, photographer / Fig. 4.9. Sarah J. Boykin, photographer / Fig. 4.10. Sarah J. Boykin / Fig. 4.11. Sarah J. Boykin, photographer / Fig. 4.12. Sarah J. Boykin, photographer / Fig. 4.13. Courtesy of Yovy Gonzalez / Fig. 4.14. Courtesy of Yovy Gonzalez / Fig. 4.15. Sarah J. Boykin, photographer / Fig. 4.16. Courtesy of Special Collections and Archives, McCain Library, Agnes Scott College / Fig. 4.17. Sarah J. Boykin, photographer / Fig. 4.18. Photograph: Scott Simpson / Fig. 4.19. Photograph: Scott Simpson / Fig. 4.20. Photograph: Scott Simpson / Fig. 4.21. Photograph: Scott Simpson / Fig. 4.22. Sarah J. Boykin / Fig. 4.23. Sarah J. Boykin, photographer / Fig. 4.24. Sarah J. Boykin, photographer / Fig. 4.25. Sarah J. Boykin, photographer / Fig. 4.26. Sarah J. Boykin, photographer.

Fig. App.1. Courtesy Woodward Academy / Fig. App.2. Thomas Roche, photographer / Fig. App.3. Daryl O'Hare Photography / Fig. App.4. Thomas Roche, photographer.

INDEX

McDonough–Adams St.–King's Highway (MAK) Historic District (Decatur, Ga.), xvii–xviii, 2, *24*, *30–32*, *40*, *106*, 107

Miller, Burd, x

minimal traditional houses, 77–81, *81–86*
 features of, 79
 McAlester on, 78, 79, 136n2
 ranch houses and, 92

Minter Homes Co., 132n11

Montgomery Ward, 13

Murphy beds, 10, 34, *36*

National Housing Act (1934), 78

New Deal policies, 78

New Homes of Quality (Wilburn), 20, 62–63
 duplexes in, 71–73, *73*
 features of, 63–64
 plan design no. 2054 in, 63–64, *64*
 plan design no. 2369 in, *73*
 plan design no. 2551 in, 71–73, *73*, 85
 plan design no. 3856 in, *65*
 smaller designs in, 77

New Plans for Home Builders (Wilburn), 20

Newton, Jean League, 11

Oliphant, William Franklin, 11

One-Story Houses (Wilburn), 20

"Own Your Own Home" movement, 4, 6, 51
 affordability and, 23, 65, 77

Padgett and Sons architectural firm, xvi, 9–11, 125, 133n21

Palladian windows, 59, *60*

Palliser and Palliser architectural firm, ix, 12

Peters Building (Atlanta), xvi–xvii, *xvii*, 11, 15, 89

Piedmont and 3rd Condominiums, 127, *128*

Piedmont Park Apartments (Atlanta), 74, 126–27, *127*

plan books, 9–12, 17–24, 64–65, 104, 105, 133n32
 advantages of, 19, 21
 advertisements in, *14*, *15*, *18*, *36*
 advertising of, 1, *6*, 16
 history of, 11–12
 lumber and mill lists with, 19–20, 28
 mail-order catalogues versus, x
 prices of, 11, 16, 20, 74, 85
 specifications of, *28*

Ponce de Leon Terrace (Decatur), 8, 58

porches, 8, 29–31, *29–31*, 51
 cross-gabled, *40*, *45*, 50, *60–61*, *72*, 99, *100*
 minimal traditional houses with, 79
 sleeping, xii, 2, 25, *38*, *54*

porte cochere, 44, 59, *60*, 75

post-Victorian southern homes, 76

prairie-style houses, 25–26, 65, 135n7

prefabricated houses, 13
 See also ready-cut house catalogues

prices
 of builders, xi, 7, 28
 of custom designs, 19
 of design plans, 11, 16, 20, 74, 85

Principles for Planning Small Houses (FHA), 78–80

Queen Anne style, 12

Radford Architectural Co., x

Ragland, E., 128

Ramsey, David, 137n1

Ranch and Colonial Homes (Wilburn), 20, 22, *91–97*, 91–98
 cover of, *91*
 plan design no. 1961 in, 92, *93*
 plan design no. 2062 in, 94, *95*
 plan design no. 2145 in, 92, *93*
 plan design no. 2247 in, *91*
 plan design no. 2268 in, 96, *97*
 plan design no. 2346 in, 92–94, *94*
 plan design no. 2566 in, 94–96, *96*
 plan design no. 3154 in, 94, *95*
 See also colonial revival–style houses

ranch houses, 20, 77
 features of, 91–92
 minimal traditional houses and, 92

ready-cut house catalogues, x–xi, 12–13

Reiff, Daniel D., 11–12, 133n31

Richardson, Mrs. Alonzo, 125–26

Rosslyn Apartments (Atlanta), 74, *126*

Schweitzer, Robert, 134n39

Sears Roebuck and Co., x, 6, 13

Sixty Good New Homes (Wilburn), 20, *86–90*, 86–91
 built-in furnishings of, 87
 colonial–revival style houses in, 86–89, *87–89*
 cover of, *86*
 plan design no. 1243 in, 86, *87*
 plan design no. 1534 in, 87, *88*
 plan design no. 1666 in, 87–89, *89*
 plan design no. 1774 in, 89, *90*

plan design no. 2085 in, *86*

and sleeping porches, xii, 2, 25, *38*, *54*

Small Low-Cost Homes for the South (Wilburn), 20, *79–86*, 91
 colonial revival–style houses in, 79, *81*, *82*, *86*, 87
 cover of, *79*
 innovations of, 79
 plan design no. 1096 in, *80*, 80–81
 plan design no. 1178 in, *81*
 plan design no. 1231 in, *81*
 plan design no. 1341 in, 83, *84*, *86*
 plan design no. 1739 in, *81*, *82*
 plan design no. 1851 in, *82*
 plan design no. 1856 in, 85, *86*
 plan design no. 1991 in, 117–22, *120–23*
 plan design no. 2065 in, 81–83, *83*
 plan design no. 2569 in, 83–85, *85*

Southern Association of Science and Industry, 125

Southern Homes and Bungalows (Wilburn), xi, xviii, 2, 26, 36, 132n3
 advertisements in, *14*, *15*
 built-in furnishings of, 32, 34–39, *37–40*
 and climatic considerations, 25, 34
 cover of, *4*
 and craftsman style, *35*, 107, *108–10*, *126*
 duplexes in, 67–70, *70*
 features of, 32
 introduction to, 2
 plan design no. 587 in, 34, *35*
 plan design no. 609 in, 32, *33*